Parenting Teens

A Guidebook for Parents and Caregivers

(How to Create a True Family Connection)

Donald Magee

Published by Rob Miles

© **Donald Magee**

All Rights Reserved

Parenting Teens: A Guidebook for Parents and Caregivers
(How to Create a True Family Connection)

ISBN 9781990084362

All rights reserved. No part of this guide may be reproduced in any form without permission in writing from the publisher except in the case of brief quotations embodied in critical articles or reviews.

Legal & Disclaimer

The information contained in this book is not designed to replace or take the place of any form of medicine or professional medical advice. The information in this book has been provided for educational and entertainment purposes only.

The information contained in this book has been compiled from sources deemed reliable, and it is accurate to the best of the Author's knowledge; however, the Author cannot guarantee its accuracy and validity and cannot be held liable for any errors or omissions. Changes are periodically made to this book. You must consult your doctor or get professional medical advice before using any of the suggested remedies, techniques, or information in this book.

Upon using the information contained in this book, you agree to hold harmless the Author from and against any damages, costs, and expenses, including any legal fees potentially resulting from the application of any of the information provided by this guide. This disclaimer applies to any damages or injury caused by the use and application, whether directly or indirectly, of any advice or information presented, whether for breach of contract, tort, negligence, personal injury, criminal intent, or under any other cause of action.

You agree to accept all risks of using the information presented inside this book. You need to consult a professional medical practitioner in order to ensure you are both able and healthy enough to participate in this program.

Table of Contents

INTRODUCTION 1

CHAPTER 1: SINGLE DADS: YOU'RE NOT ALONE 4

CHAPTER 2: TIPS FOR BEING A GOOD STEP PARENT 10

CHAPTER 3: BEHAVIOR MODIFICATION THEORY 16

CHAPTER 4: RULES OF NO-DRAMA DISCIPLINE: THE 3 C'S, CONNECTION, COMMUNICATION, COOPERATION 22

CHAPTER 5: NATURE VS. NURTURE 32

CHAPTER 6: HAVING FUN WITH TODDLERS 46

CHAPTER 7: HOW DO I HELP MY TEENAGER THROUGH DIFFICULT TRANSITIONS (DIVORCE, LOSS OF A LOVED ONE, COMING OUT, ETC?) 54

CHAPTER 8: YOUR CHILD'S HEALTH AND NUTRITION 62

CHAPTER 9: LESSON ON COMMUNICATING WITH YOUR KIDS 77

CHAPTER 10: MAKING A STATEMENT WITHOUT 'RAISING YOUR VOICE' 85

CHAPTER 11: NEWBORN BABIES 90

- CHAPTER 12: HOW DADS CAN USURP THE POWER OF PEER-PRESSURE? 103
- CHAPTER 13: BOOBY TRAPS TO AVOID 114
- CHAPTER 14: RAISING AN OPTIMISTIC CHILD 120
- CHAPTER 15: BACKTALK 124
- CHAPTER 16: BE THE ROLE MODEL & INSTILL GOOD MANNERS 134
- CHAPTER 17: MANAGING FINANCES 140
- CHAPTER 18: COMMON BEHAVIOR CONCERNS 153
- CHAPTER 19: HOW TO REPLACE PUNISHMENT WITH POSITIVE PARENTING 170
- CHAPTER 20: BUILDING RESILIENCY 181
- CHAPTER 21: MAKING YOUR CHILD FEEL SAFE AND SECURED 186
- CHAPTER 22: SINGLE MOM WITH TODDLER - CUTTING TOXIC TV TIME 194
- CONCLUSION 201

Introduction

There is nothing more terrific, nor more terrifying, than finding out you are going to be a new Dad. Man, it's the best, scariest news a man could ever hear. While you are no doubt thrilled, you are also probably shaking in your boots. Don't worry. It's perfectly normal. In fact, these mixed emotions can pretty well sum the eighteen or so years that lie ahead. The good news is that with a little help from this book, you'll get through them all with flying colors.

First, congratulations! Your life is about to change. You will never be the same. You are going to be a "pro" at fatherhood. I know that because I'm going to show you how to be one.

From the time you were drafted (also known as conception), the little life that has been growing is your all-star player. Just as team owners, managers and coaches all learn their duties by way of both teachings and experience, so will you. I'm giving you this blueprint, your game book so that you can handle your plays accordingly. When coupled with your real-life lessons, you are sure to come out winning.

So... you don't have a clue how to put a diaper on your baby? That's pretty much a given, especially if you've never had or been around a baby (you likely haven't diapered someone else's kid). With that said, you now do have a reason to learn. Any good Dad should know how to put a diaper on his own child. Within the pages of this book, you will learn all the basics. You'll learn how easy it is not only to diaper your little one, but also to feed him, bath him and effectively communicate with him.

Not only will you learn the tricks of the trade with your baby, you'll be schooled in some helpful hints about enhancing your relationship with his mother. The two of you will grow stronger because of the baby you share… if you do a few simple things mentioned in this book.

Having a baby is scary. For instance, they can be pint-sized nightmares if you don't know how to comfort and soothe them. Your relationship with his mother can fall apart overnight. You can wake up with a two year-old you barely know and a woman with whom you share a child but not much else. Don't let that happen to you. Reading this book may be the single best thing you can do for yourself and your new family.

What makes a good Dad? Keep reading—learn about the first three years of your baby's life and how you can be a huge part of it. Be a life-changing winning father simply by following some of the book's suggestions. But don't wait. The time is now to make the plays that will ultimately win the game. Take the ball, run and by all means, read this book!

Chapter 1: Single Dads: You're Not Alone

By definition, a single dad refers to a father who gained sole custody of his child (**or children as the case may be**) following a family change or breakup. The family change can be a divorce, death of a spouse, or separation from a partner.

Whatever the underlying circumstance may be, the single dad is often left desolated – completely overwhelmed by guilt, anger, or depression following the unplanned family change. Single dads also come under extreme pressures from outside the family circle - they are discriminated against at work, left out in social circles, and rarely get child support. A number of them feel they have been abandoned even by family and friends.

But if it is of any consolation to the single dad, it may help him to know that he is not alone in this dire predicament. There are almost 2.5 million other single dads in the

US taking the same route to single fatherhood, which **is more than double the numbers 10 years ago**--and this statistic is increasing every year.

The 2.5 million single dads in the country today come in all shades of gray. There are single dads resulting from divorce; single dads whose wives have died; and single dads who separated from their non-marital partners they were co-habiting with. In some rare cases there are single dads by choice who became fathers through surrogacy.

The common denominator among all these single dads is they have sole custody of their children. In other words, the double responsibilities of going to work in order to provide for the material needs of their children and spending time to care for the kids' emotional, intellectual, and spiritual welfare rest exclusively on their shoulders.

This is not an easy mantle for single dads to play considering the fact that the traditional role they play in the family is that of a provider, while child care has historically been the responsibility of wives or partners. With the family change however, single dads now have to balance work with child care, which, more often than not, leads to neglecting one or the other. The bad news is if even for a short period of time single dads neglect any or both of these responsibilities, it can have grave consequences on their children's future.

Let me tell you why. There are studies that say that children from single parent households exhibit the most violent behaviors (**including suicide**). There are also statistics that say **60% of those who commit rape and 72% of teenage murderers come from single parent households**. These shocking figures underscore the need for single dads to walk the extra mile and exhaust all available options to meet the challenges of single fatherhood broadly and squarely –

or, they risk having their own children added up to these numbers.

Sadly, single dads often find themselves overwhelmed with anger or depression after a breakup (or after being widowed) so much so that they start developing feelings of guilt which distracts them from attending to the real responsibilities of single fatherhood. Immobilized by grief, guilt, or sometimes fear of failure in tackling the enormous responsibilities ahead, they start blaming themselves for being single parents. Worst, they try to make up for this by spoiling their children.

Overcoming the anger, the depression, or the feeling of guilt is therefore the most important '**first thing task**' single dads have to attend to before they are able to move on to the more crucial task of child rearing. They can't be effective at parenting if they continue to sulk in their misfortunes. They have to rid themselves of the negative vibes and create a more positive environment to raise their young children properly.

This, unfortunately, is easier said than done. It is not like just waking up the next morning with a clean slate and with all the problems gone. It takes a lot and it takes a while to heal the wounds of a family break up. Suddenly thrown into the arena of single parenting without prior preparation or knowledge of what lies ahead, most single dads often drown in the stream of single parenting challenges that will surely engulf him right from day one.

There is some good news though for single dads - they don't have to go through the trials and tribulation of single parenting alone. They can draw strength and inspiration from other single dads around them. They can also solicit the help of family and friends who I without a doubt will be more than willing to aid them get through their ordeals. There are also tons of single dad resources that can be found online (**like this book**) which they can always tap anytime. Better still, there are single dad networks and single parent organizations they can depend on for much needed support should they require some. And, all they need to do is to reach out.

If you are a single dad, rejoice. You are not alone!

Chapter 2: Tips For Being A Good Step Parent

Become acquainted with the kids before you take your promises. Turning into a step family can be a troublesome move for everybody, except it helps an awesome arrangement if potential step parents have the chance to shape friendly associations with their partner's kids before they join as a family.

Comprehend that the kids are a lasting portion of your life. Youngsters and the intricacies that join them are never a rare phenomenon. Regardless of where the kids call home, parents and step parents must be set up to settle on a considerable lot of their life decisions taking into account the requirements of the kids.

Try not to expect instantaneous love. Minding connections require some serious energy to grow, so great step parents permit their step children a lot of time to acclimate to their nearness in their family.

Solicit regard. While step children ought not to be compelled to pretend adoration for a step parent, they ought to be required to carry on in a deferential way.

Be benevolent and reliable. A standout for the most imperative principles of being a parent is to practice consideration and consistency. Great parents and step parents comprehend the estimation of furnishing children with a strong home base.

Acknowledge your step children for who they are. Parents do not get the opportunity to pick the kind of kids that they get; so great step parents figure out how to acknowledge and value their step children for the uncommon people that they are and to praise every kid's distinctive blessings.

Work with your life partner as a group. House standards can be troublesome for youngsters to acknowledge, however, when they are exhibited by both the kids' parent and step parent, kids understand that they will be required to go along.

Try not to rival the youngsters for your life partner's affection or time. A parent ought to dependably apportion time to go through with their kids. Certain step parents understand that their life partner's affection for their youngsters not the slightest bit reduces their relationship.

Support your marriage. Much of the time, step children have needed to persevere through the difficult separation of their folks' relationship. They do not have to remember that agony by seeing the end of their parent and step parent's marriage.

Never reprimand your life partner before the kids. This standard applies pretty much as similarly to normal kids.

Try not to talk about custody or child support before the kids. Children ought not to be subjected to differences between their folks and ought to be protected, however, much as could reasonably be expected from grown-up issues.

Try not to sweat over small things. Figuring out how to pick fights astutely and to evade insignificant contentions is a certain indication of a decent step parent.

Be an adult. Silly or narrow-minded conduct has no spot in child rearing.

Try not to be hesitant to say no. Kids need to live by a sensible arrangement of principles, so great step parents discover the quality to take a firm stand when the welfare of the kids is in question.

Treat the greater part of the kids similarly. Regular youngsters and step children ought to be relied upon to firmly stick to the same arrangement of house standards and must be provided the same benefits.

Approach your partner's ex with deference. Treating the kids' other regular parent rudely is destructive to the children and is never alright.

Get used to sharing occasions and other unique days. Kids have more family than just the individuals who live in their family, so concessions must be made to see that the kids have admittance to their other relatives.

Make a sheltered domain that permits the genuine sharing of sentiments. While children ought not to be permitted to treat other relatives unkindly, they ought to be permitted and urged to express their feelings, realizing that their emotions will be considered important.

Exercise persistence. Being a decent step parent regularly requires a lot of tolerance. Kids, however great, can be taxing and savvy step parents know when to step back and a take couple of full breaths.

20. Keep in mind that science is not the most vital part about being a parent. The most

imperative of the greater part of the tenets, this one is a gentle reminder about what is

really vital in any family, and that is affection. The most valuable bonds are not those of

coordinating strands of DNA, but rather of an existence shared.

Chapter 3: Behavior Modification Theory

Encouraging The Good, Discouraging The Bad

This is simple. Any behavior that is reinforced by rewards will tend to be repeated. So apart from using voice tones and discipline techniques, you also reward a repeat and positive performance.

Behavior modification also has a reverse side stating that any good behavior that goes unnoticed or unacknowledged will only disappear in the process. Children need to be reassured all the time. They need constant encouragement to know that they are doing well. In toddlers, behavior modification will work best if the good behavior gets to be rewarded in an instant. This technique must be used consistently in order for it to become effective. On the other hand, if bad behavior is going to be ignored and underplayed just so your child knows that he has no audience to impress, you may allow four to five occurrences before doing something about the behavior.

The Rewards

Rewarding toddlers for a job well done regardless if it is about behaving well in public places or getting along well with other kids should be performed because that is just how things are. Put it this way, you get rewarded with money for working, you get extra pay for extra work, or your older kids get good grades for studying hard. Simply put, if rewarding adults is thought appropriate, why not children, right?

The Soft Rewards

These refer to rewards that primarily makes use of attention, smile, touch, praises, hugs and kisses. When used wisely and cautiously, this can be all powerful and effective. When misused, it could promote undesirable behaviors. Toddlers are sensitive to this kind of reward, and they often give in to these simply because they love being praised, cuddled, and noticed by their parents given their age.

The Hard Rewards

These can be in the form of items such as a star stamp, smiley sticker, or a "good job" chart. These work for children who are in their preschool. You may also want to give them sweet treats and other kiddie stuff.

Soft or Hard Rewards? Which one is best?

When deciding whether to go for soft or hard rewards, your child's age is an important factor to consider. Toddlers are more content with soft rewards while older toddlers are more enticed with the idea of having stickers or sweets if they behaved well. Just remember that the very purpose of behavior modification is to reward a good behavior that has happened. You shouldn't do this by offering them the reward beforehand as eventually they will start asking or expecting an incentive before they do anything. This technique will help you steer a challenging and stubborn toddler around without ruining your already demanding day.

Another common example of behavior modification is when it comes to feeding. Toddlers are picky eaters or would rather not eat at all. As with this behavior modification, what a parent like you must do is put the food in front of your toddler. He either picks up or eats the food, or he ends up hungry and asks for a bottle of milk. You do not insist, do airplane noises, juggles fruits, or scold at your child. You just let him decide what he is going to do with the food. If he eats, then good for the both of you. But when he rejects, just ignore. There is a higher chance that he will end up eating the food. Now, that is maintained sanity and no future fights over food. Also, children can start to relate eating with stress which can lead to all types of problems so meal time should not be a big deal to them.

Changes will come little y little

You do not devise a behavior plan and apply it to your child all convinced that it will work only after hours of doing it. Behavior modifications would take time and practice. There is no point expecting a child to instantly transform himself from being untamed to a refined one. You have to allow weeks and months to see the real change.

As you utilize behavior modifications, you have to remember to keep your defenses strong and show that there is a new you who is in charge and means business. Sometimes, you even have to put up with a bit of extra pain in order to reap long-term rewards. If you are dedicated to making this technique work for your child, you have to be prepared to handle and go through dark and difficult times before you finally see results, good results.

Smacking just won't cut it

Smacking or using force against a child as a form of discipline is wrong. While there are those who resort to occasional smack, there are also those who frequently beat their children. Remember, this will set a bad example to children and will remember unhappy experiences when they grow up. Children also learn from you if you resort to violence when you can't solve a problem, it is likely that they will start to think the same

Chapter 4: Rules Of No-Drama Discipline: The 3 C's, Connection, Communication, Cooperation

The 3 C's are your godsends in parenting. They are connection, communication, and cooperation. When you run into problems with your child, take a deep breath and remember the 3 C's.

Connection

The parent-child bond is one that will shape your child's entire life. It is a sacred bond, but it can become strained with personality clashes, fighting, and anger. Your relationship may even get dull, which is inevitable when you spend as much time with a person as you do your child. However, keeping the bond sacred and close is the best way to keep a high level of affection with your child, even in the tense or bad times. It will also pay off in adulthood, when you become your child's best friend and number one confidante.

There are many ways to keep the connection strong and alive. Here are a few ideas:

Play word games, board games, and unstructured games in the open air. Make silly faces and play dress-up. Play is how children learn to be people.

Laugh together. Humor reduces resistance and causes you to share smiles. Inside jokes are especially bonding.

Read together. This causes your child to look to you for information and ask you questions as you open the world for your child.

Pay more attention to the child than to his actions. Get to know who your child is. This is not hard to do – simply listen to what he shares about himself as you share meals, read together, and play together.

Communication

The root of resistance and other problems often is in miscommunication between adult and child. This is because it is hard to bridge the gap in intellect and ideas, when adults and children have different worlds inside their heads. Getting to know your child's plans, dreams, problems, worries, and preferences can help you avoid the clashes that arise when you are on different pages mentally.

Your child cannot yet communicate as you do. Therefore, you cannot blame him for not telling you certain things, because he has no idea how. It is your job to set the model to teach him how to communicate. It falls to you to maintain communication at first. Over time, he will develop the skills to communicate properly back with you.

Here are some tips to make communicating across the maturity gap a bit easier:

Listen with your heart. Don't just take what your child says at face value. Actually observe his body language, facial expressions, and actions to figure out what he's really feeling and thinking. You know his mental process pretty well since you have been through childhood yourself. Just use some empathy and remember your own childhood to glean clues into what he cannot phrase yet. Then offer him a listening ear and don't offer advice unless he asks.

Think, connect, and redirect the child. Consider this example: your child is throwing a fit because you said no to cookies after he brushed his teeth. Start by acknowledging what he feels by saying, "I heard you. You're upset because you want cookies. " That lets him know you understand his feelings and prevents the frustration and acting out he may engage in if he feels as if his emotions are not being heard. Then reconnect with him by saying, "I love cookies too!" Finally, propose a reasonable solution, such as picking some cookies and eating them the next day at the park.

Make a firm resolution not to use punishment to control your child. This only breeds resentment, which leads to your child acting out and feeling free of responsibility. Instead of punishing and controlling him, teach him to make good decisions and take responsibility.

Praise your child and tell him good things about himself. If you criticize him constantly, you make him believe that nothing he does is good enough, so why bother trying? You may criticize him more than you think. So make a list of his good points and read the list to him every day. Have him list his own strengths and good traits as well. Reward him for good behavior and the positive aspects of his personality rather than criticize his "bad" traits or punish the negative things he does. This grows healthy self-esteem in your child.

"No" is not a complete thought. Spell out your reasoning so he understands why you said no. Then he can't argue.

Children will act out when they are upset. Their bad behavior can be a reflection of something unrelated, such as a divorce or being bullies at school. Don't just punish his bad behavior. Actually try to direct him to speak about his feelings in a healthy way rather than taking them out on others with poor behavior and disobedience. If he doesn't want to talk at first, don't take it personally. He may not know how to phrase how he is actually feeling. Tell him you are there for him and that you won't get mad no matter what he tells you, in order to leave the door open for communication.

Speak to him politely. This will teach him a model for how to speak to others. Rudeness is not inherent, but rather learned.

Cooperation

For harmony in this relationship, you must cooperate together as a partnership or a family team. Everyone must be on board and they must all work together toward a common goal. Encouraging cooperation requires kindness, patience, and positive reinforcement. You won't enable cooperation if you are always berating, criticizing, or punishing your child and making him fear or resent you.

Here are some tips to bring about maximum cooperation within your family:

Treat your child as a person with his own thoughts and feelings. Include him in discussions and get his input. Acknowledge what he says, even if you disagree with it.

Do not view your child's disobedience as a personal insult. Instead, view it as a problem you can solve together. Say he's throwing a fit about going to bed. Realize that he is doing this because he has his own goals and wants to be doing something other than sleeping. Tell him, "I can see you don't want to go to bed. What else do you want to be doing? Do you think there's a time you can do that tomorrow, so you can go to bed now and wake up feeling well-rested?" Or ask, "What can make you want to clean your room?" Then come to a solution together.

Invite him to do chores with you instead of demanding for him to do them. Then it seems like teamwork.

Set firm rules and explain them in simple language. Make it clear that no means no and he may not break the rules.

However, don't put tons of unnecessary rules on him. Strong-willed children feel suffocated by rules and will rebel. Let him have some freedom. Ask yourself, "Will this hurt me or him in any way?" Things that don't harm you or him may not need to be restricted. Give him some freedom and space to make his own self.

Develop signals with your child. These would be your own personal secret language. That way, you can signal to each other when it's time to do homework or end a discussion. You may also have a signal so he can tell you he needs to talk without interrupting your conversation with someone else. Give him a wait signal and then acknowledge his needs when there is a break in the conversation.

Build a routine together. He will demand the same of you, so follow along.

Don't fight against your child's natural tendencies. Say he is a perfectionist. Let him order his room the way he wants instead of fighting with him about how neatness and order doesn't matter so much. This lets him be himself and grow into the person he is naturally meant to be.

Should you eventually lose your temper, it's not too late. Remove your boxing gloves, take a deep breath, and say, "I'm sorry I lost my temper. Let's think of a solution together." Doing this enables him to trust you thoroughly.

Remember! Children who are born in "boxing gloves" often grow into those who change this world the most. Raising children of this magnitude is difficult, but it produces a fantastic adult who knows how to control his temper!

Chapter 5: Nature Vs. Nurture

How much of your child's inherent traits and abilities are genetic and how much can be altered?

The answer, in both cases, is quite a lot. Parenting experts (present company included) have been quoted saying that nature and nurture work hand in hand with the development of exceptional children.

Studies suggest that many behavioral and temperamental tendencies are approximately 30%-50% genetic. Five major personality traits, usually called the Big 5 have been reported to show the strongest influence:

Extroversion

Agreeableness

Neuroticism

Conscientiousness

Openness to experience

Others with a significant genetic legacy include:

Altruism

Shyness

Accident-proneness

Self-esteem

The way that you treat any child you bring up (parenting personality) appears to be far less significant than people once thought. However, what is most important are the different ways you interact with your child as an individual. Whether you like it or not, the truth of the matter is that in the end, you won't have much influence on what you'd want your child to be: be it an artist or an athlete, a do-gooder or even a go-getter, a lover of opera or a lover of jazz. Nevertheless, you can certainly help them become the best individuals they can be. Rather ironically, the more you consent and respond to each of your child's distinctive tendencies as they take place - the more you let them "set the pace," and as fate would have it, the more influence you have in their life.

Here's the new parenting mantra - Observe, encourage and indulge. This does not necessarily mean being submissive. An infant who appears excessively emotional or shy may need special care and guidance. Just don't expect to eventually "overcome" such tendencies. You should also not go overboard trying to provide your child with the "exact" opportunities and stimulation. Foster good values and set limits, however, don't panic at the thought that your child isn't going to the very best of schools, taking the right lessons or even reading the right books. All the extras so popular in our day may be of great importance. However, they won't change a child's predisposition much.

As you well know, every child has a unique temperament from the very early stages of infancy. While some infants may be calm, others may seem to have been born "kicking and screaming." Studies show that a child who exhibits difficult temperaments as an infant may have complications later in life. When a child is impulsive, short-tempered, and inattentive, they tend to express their difficulties by acting out and distancing themselves from others. Similarly, a very withdrawn and shy child may eventually develop anxiety-related disorders later in life.

Have you ever stopped to think of the effect that you may have on your child if they display challenging or difficult temperaments early in life? In most cases, the child's behavior arouses certain parent behaviors. If not carefully checked, your parental behaviors could worsen the child's tendencies, and thus end up aggravating stronger responses from you and, as a result, further escalate the temperamental problems of your child.

The bottom line remains that although your child may have been born with a challenging temperament, your quality of parenting can control the extent to which this temperament leads to difficulties later in life. It's important to note that your child's susceptibilities for mental health problems can be triggered by certain prompts, including poor parenting. Still, their strengths can be stimulated by how effective you are in your parenting. Good parenting allows a child to explore and use their characteristic abilities to the maximum.

Several studies on the progress of the "Information Age" suggest that the world is fast moving into a new era. An age of "creative innovation". You might call it the "creative age." Nurturing creativity in your child will arm you with a strong ingenious advantage over the rest of the world. If you prepare them right, your child could help shape the direction the new age takes.

So the big question is, how do you inspire your child to be more creative?

Children are born with creative imagination. Many children especially can lose that great sense of creativity if parents do not take care, as there is often pressure for strong-willed children to conform to the ideas society (especially where bad parenting is concerned).

As a parent, rather than crush or starve creativity, you need to cultivate and encourage that creative energy in your child. That is what will give them the edge in future. Also, their brain is in a state of continuous development, and those portions of the brain that make up creative ability will be much stronger and sharper and if they are exercised now.

Children and the power of improvisation

One of the simplest phases of creativity with which a child is born is improvisation. It's that impulsive energy that gets them to do an instantaneous, impromptu dance, coloring or singing. It's that instant of unrehearsed storytelling or block-building.

Any time a child does something creative spontaneous, they are indeed improvising.

Improvisation can be found almost everywhere - in music, art, make-believe, comedy, sports and just about everything in the "childhood activity" bracket. It's also at the very core of the play.

Ideas to promote creative improvisation in your young one:

Find pictures and shapes in the clouds and point them out to your child. They'll quickly catch on, and join in eagerly.

Bring stuffed animals and other toys to life. Walk your child's toys around the house and interact with the surrounding environment. You could turn their heads to look around or even have them move their feet like marionettes as they walk. Give them specific voices that will separate you from the figurine in the child's mind. Have their head turn free of their body to look at your child, and make their hands move as a puppet might move. This will definitely catch their attention.

When your child wants to color, get them a blank page rather than a coloring book. This will go a long way into nurturing their artistic development. Children love to color, thus give yours lots of opportunities to draw something from nothing. Better yet, do join them with your writing material and paper. They'll watch what you come up with and imitate your style. Just make sure they are stimulated to use their creativity instead of always requiring your assistance.

Have a storytelling table, rug or chair. Whoever is on this chair tells everyone a story. Who doesn't love a good story? But rather than always having to get out the picture book, make it a point of telling them from your own head one in a while. You could even invent them on the spot - creativity. If your creativity was squelched in your younger years, you are going to have problems doing this part. You could also learn to recite some spur-of-the-moment stories. But don't always be the one to tell them. Inspire your children to tell their stories, ones that they come up with from their heads and let them do it without your help.

Schedule some dancing sessions. There is a natural tendency in human beings to want to move to music. While society may squelch that, take it upon yourself to nurture it in your child. Turn on some tune, start dancing, and get your children to join you and in the process help them come up with their own dance moves. The dance hall could be your own living room, back yard or even your bedroom. Doing so will not only nurture your child's creativity, but it will also give you a little much-needed exercise.

Learn to parent purposefully so that your child can display and grow their own creative artistic brilliance. It is NOT about hot-housing your child or having them jump years ahead at school.

Children are born lively, curious and nosy. All too often in mid-childhood, the primary fires of genius that scorched so radiantly fade, and there is a risk that they will be quenched out. If this happens, a child fears trying out new things and worry about making mistakes. The child is left with an inhibited version of their capabilities and even themselves.

Luckily, the power of parents to kindle the fire of genius at this time becomes really inspiring. You have at your fingertips the best workshop for cracking your child's brilliance - it's called the world. By playing, creating and exploring it, you can expand your child's mind. By taking time with it to enjoy, wonder, and be curious, you kindle a blaze that will flicker and flourish forever in your child's life.

It takes great confidence to be a child. From going to a new school, to stepping up to bat for the first time, children face many unfamiliar terrains. Naturally, as a parent, you want to impart a can-do attitude in your child so that they'll fearlessly take on new challenges and, over time, have confidence in themselves. While each child is a little different, parents can with no doubt build their children' confidence.

Self-confidence stems out of a sense of aptitude. In other words, children cultivate confidence not because their parents tell them they're great, but because of their accomplishments, both big and small. Sure, it's good to hear reassuring words from both mom and dad. Nevertheless, words of approval mean more when they refer to a child's particular willpower or new abilities.

When your child achieves something, whether it's riding a bike or brushing their teeth, they feel themselves as capable and knowledgeable and tap into the fuel of confidence.

Building confidence in your child can begin very early. When tots learn to take their very first steps or babies learn to turn the pages of a book, they are getting the idea - "I can do it!" With each new milestone and skill, your child can develop increasing self-confidence.

You can help your child become confident by giving them opportunities to exercise and master their skills. Let your child make mistakes and still be there to boost their spirits so they keep trying. Respond interestedly and excitedly when your child shows off a new skill, and reward them with compliments when they realize set goals or make a good effort.

With good instruction, abundant opportunities and lots of patience from you, your child can master basic skills such as tying their shoes and making their bed. Then, when other vital challenges present themselves, your child will approach them knowing that they have already been successful in other areas.

Nurturing Independence in your child

Many children enter pre-school without the slightest idea of how to open containers, feed themselves, pour a drink, work buttons or even put things into a bag. When their teacher asks them to get their backpack or lunch box, some children have no idea, how to perform simple tasks independently. You will indeed help your child a great deal if you let them select their own backpack and lunch bag. Go the extra mile of even showing them how to label their items. Show them the how to use the potty correctly and then stand back and let them do it themselves.

As the old axiom goes "Practice Makes Perfect", this has never been truer as you watch your child learn how to tie a shoelace. Make sure their clothes fit comfortably and that they can handle any zippers or buttons. Make sure that they always know which shoe goes on which foot.

Independence gives them pride and self-confidence in their ability. Independence lets them know that you believe in them to care for their belongings, make the right decisions and that they are set and ready for the next big phase of their development. Strong-willed children sometimes strive to assert their independence. By creating sufficient opportunities for children to be independent, many parents have alleviated a lot of the stress of raising strong -willed children by giving them an outlet to assert their sense of independence and individuality.

Chapter 6: Having Fun With Toddlers

When your baby hits a year old, they're officially called "toddlers". This is the cutest, most adorable, most nerve-wrecking and hyperactive time of their life. It is a period of great cognitive, physical, social, and emotional development and close parent monitoring is a must. It's not like you're going to have to be told to do it anyway, you're going to love your child so much that at this point you wouldn't want to take your eyes off them. So what really happens and how do you keep up with it?

The Magical First Word

On the average, the toddler learns to speak his first word during the first year, however for some cases it can take as long as 3 years, so don't fret. Even the world's smartest person, Einstein, didn't speak a word until he was 3.

It is a common myth that the earlier a child learns to talk, the smarter he is.

Children simply have different paces of learning. You can encourage your toddler to talk by making regular two-way communication with them and making sure to slow down so your toddler keeps up. But really, no pressure, they'll figure it out eventually.

Physical development and the power of play

Toddlers are tireless. They can go on running and jumping about all day and that's actually good! They're actually hard at work in developing physical skills by learning muscle control and coordination. They're like sponges that can absorb everything they see, hear, feel, and sense. It's a brilliant time to take advantage of this phase in their lives to teach them key values and skills. Here are a couple of ways to make take advantage of their playtime.

Toddlers don't care about price tags — anything that beeps, lights up, and moves will instantly catch their attention. It can get really funny when you see your kids hold on to an improvised car while completely ignoring a newly minted toy after less than a minute. If you think about it that can really help your budget!

Encourage outdoor activity – it is good to expose kids to the outside world early on, and let them experience the joys of running around and playing with kids they've only met. Yes they will get dirty, yes they will probably wound themselves in the process, but that's part of learning! As they grow up, their healthy outdoor life will occupy their fondest memories, more than sitting in one corner playing with their Android.

Unleash their inner Picasso – even small activities like drawing a circle or a coloring a tree requires muscle activity, and sharpens up their motor skills. Childhood is a great time to explore and let their creativity loose. This allows them to exercise decision making, say in what color they'd like to use or how they'd like their drawings to look like.

Pretend play – the power of make believe is in full swing when kids are still small and you wouldn't believe how wild their imagination could get. Try to discover the world they have created instead of ignoring it, and you will learn a lot about how your child processes the things he sees.

Getting Rid of the Tantrum Scare

Your toddler may look like a tiny little doll, but their emotional needs are much larger than most adults, mainly because find it hard to communicate how they truly feel. This is the point when they are starting to realize that they are a separate being from their parent, that they can make things happen and therefore begin to explore and test limits in their own scale. They struggle between trying to figure things out on their own, and their immense attachment to the people they love. This can cause a lot of anxiety and insecurity on the kid, which is translated into bursting emotion yet still lacking the ability to properly communicate via the spoken language. These bursts of emotion aren't just about tantrums but also happen in bursts of love. One moment their screaming inconsolably and the next moment they chuckle and shower you with kisses. Learning how a toddler perceives things is a great way to win them and reduce your stress, here's how:

Learn to be consistent – The key to giving security to toddlers is establishing their daily routines and sticking to it. They are at the point of exploring so many new things that they need assurance that their home is a safe haven where they know what will happen next.

While sticking to a schedule is easier said than done, this will save you many episodes of embarrassment. Should you need to change something, like if a visitor comes over, tell your toddler about it beforehand to set his mind. Kids understand more than we give them credit for.

This works the same for discipline. If you said "no" when he slammed the door yesterday, you must say "no" when he does it today, tomorrow, and next week. Or else this will confuse him and think that maybe next time he'll get away with it again.

Acknowledge their feelings and allow them choices – try to involve them in daily decisions like what color of shirt to wear, what pair of shoes, and et cetera. When they know that they are being acknowledged, and learn the decision-making process that comes with it, it is easier for them to understand why they can't have their way sometimes.

Try to keep your emotions at bay – Nothing good will happen from a screaming match between the two of you. Show your toddler that you're in firm control of the situation. Sometimes you will have to completely ignore them until they realize that no amount of screaming will get them another hour in front of the TV when its bedtime.

Take advantage of their short attention span — screaming because he wanted another taco? Carry him to his favorite pony and play with him; chances are he'll forget about the taco in no time. That, my friends, is the art of distraction; it can save you in many ways.

Praise them for good behavior — sometimes a kid will do what annoys you only to get attention. Other times, the impression of "bad" is most vivid in his brain because it's all you ever talk about. Capitalize on the good, a couple of rewards for every good deed will do the trick. Chances are he'll want to do something good again because he likes the feeling of his parents being proud of them.

Do this cautiously though, don't overdo it to the extent of giving rewards for every move he makes because that misses the point of good behavior. You also don't want to raise kids who are too full of themselves when they grow up, so you must balance between capitalizing on the good they have done, while being able to firmly reprimand when they do bad.

Chapter 7: How Do I Help My Teenager Through Difficult Transitions (Divorce, Loss Of A Loved One, Coming Out, Etc?)

Life is full of transitions, and when they happen during the teenage years, they can be that much more difficult for you and for them. So what are you supposed to do when you are helping your teen deal with these sorts of changes in their lives? Here are some "transition specific" answers that you can utilize in your particular circumstances.

Divorce. Divorce can be especially hard for a teenager to go through, because, in the world of a teenager, the family may feel like the only stable thing that they have. If that falls apart, then it may cause your teenager to have issues with self-esteem, emotional issues, and more. You need to make sure that your teenager completely understands the reasons behind the divorce. One issue that many teenagers (and children in general) have is that they believe that the divorce has something to do with them.

Do everything in your power to help them realize the untruth in that belief, and help them walk through any of the feelings or frustrations that they may be feeling. Let them know that both parents still love them as much as they always have. It's no one's fault that you are getting divorced; if you are in a place where you can talk about the exact reasons, go ahead and do it. Your teenager is old enough to understand your thought process. It also helps to establish trust; if you can trust them with the exact reasons for the divorce; they'll feel like they can trust you with how they're feeling about it. If you can, sit down with your child(ren) and both parents. That way, everyone is involved in the conversation and the story is one fluid story.

Even if you don't love each other anymore, you have to keep some stability for your children. That doesn't mean that you have to stay together; focus on healing yourself, but also focus on keeping your children in a safe place where they are seeing both parents on a regular basis (granted, there are cases that you don't want this to occur; cases where a spouse is abusive or incarcerated will have to be treated differently than this). Be flexible with visitations, figure out holidays, and try and make the transition as seamless as possible. That way, your children will be able to get through it without a lot of stress.

Loss of a loved one. Losing a loved one is horrible, no matter what age you're at. But if it happens to a teenager, it's that much more difficult. Not only is someone that they love gone forever, they are also face-to-face with something that usually doesn't cross the mind of a teenager: mortality. In a child's mind, a person is always there. They don't just disappear, and if they do, they always come back. As you grow into a teenager, you understand that that isn't always the case. But, that realization doesn't become reality until they lose someone close to them. Because of this, losing someone can be incredibly traumatic for your teenager to work through.

When your teenager loses a loved one (in most cases you will lose a loved one at the same time; there may be cases that this doesn't occur), the big thing that you need to do is be flexible. I know of a family that lost their mom. The older child was in her twenties, but the younger one was only 17. Their dad had a lot of struggles with the 17 year old during that first year, and the older child had to really help out in a number of ways. Their dad wanted everything to go the way that it was going before mom died, but it was difficult. The 17 year old ended up getting his GED instead of finishing school. Even though it wasn't what their dad wanted, he decided to be flexible after their mom had died.

I tell that story because, there are times that you may need to compromise so that your teenagers can cope. The above example was an extreme case that also involved a severe bout of depression that the 17 year old went through, but your case may be similar. If your child has to miss a few days of school to mourn, let them do it. If they have to go stay with a friend for a few days so that they're away from the situation, let them do it. Allow them to orchestrate their mourning; that way, you won't add the pressure and stress that can come as a result of losing someone you love. Be flexible, be there to talk to, and just love them. Those sound simple, but they are the best things that you can do during the mourning process.

"Coming Out." Please know that this doesn't only refer to sexuality in this context, even though that is the most common type of coming out that you will see. Coming out, in this sense, is talking about the times that your teenager finds a part of their personality or self that they haven't let others know about. Obviously, coming out of the closet is in the forefront; admitting that your sexuality is "different" than that of their peers can be a traumatizing experience for any teenager, especially if they are concerned about coming out to you. There are still people in this world that will not accept them for who they are; whether it's because of religious beliefs, or "the way they were raised," people can be unnecessarily cruel to those who are different than them. And as you know, this doesn't only apply to sexuality; it can apply to interests, to beliefs, to personality traits, and anything else that isn't in the "mainstream." So what can you do in those cases, especially if it is something that you have particular thoughts about?

First, you need to realize that the way that you react to their announcement, no matter what it is, is important to them. If you get upset or freak out, they're going to be less likely to share other information with you in the future. If you listen to and embrace your child just as they are, you will be more likely to see success with the conversation. Even if you don't agree with their choices, you need to show that you love them and appreciate them, just as they are. If it's something that is not inherently dangerous, then don't try to fight with them about it. Obviously, if their life choices are something that is dangerous (drugs, alcohol, etc), you're going to want to discourage them from pursuing it, but most of the time, "coming out" doesn't involve those sorts of things. Whatever their life choice may be, you want to ask them what influenced them in that direction, and what they want or expect from you as a result. It's about mutual understanding.

If you think that you won't be able to do this, then you will need to find support so that you can. Talk with your spouse, find a support group, look for more information online, and just learn with them. They're just as confused (or more so) than you are, so you have to show patience and acceptance. It will take time, but it will be worth the investment if you want to maintain the relationship through this transitioning period of time.

In all of these cases, you may need to seek professional help for your teenager (and maybe even for you) so that they can get through the transitions in a safe and healthy way. We talk more about therapy and other ways to deal with emotional struggles and mood changes in the answer to the next section; keep reading for more information on that.

Chapter 8: Your Child's Health And Nutrition

Top 5 Toddler Nutrition Musts

1. Milk

Milk is an excellent source of calcium and protein. It is also a great source of phosphorous, B-complex vitamins, as well as magnesium and Vitamins A and D. Toddlers need the fats that are contained in full cream milk, which means non-fat and low-fat milk are not recommended. If your toddler is bored of drinking milk every single day, you can try to improve such as adding strawberry flavoring or a teaspoon or two of chocolate.

2. Vegetables

Green leafy vegetables contain folacin, iron and calcium, while yellow vegetables are rich in Vitamin A. It can be quite difficult to convince toddlers to eat vegetables. It's a good idea to offer small amounts of dip with vegetables or use yogurt instead.

3. Fruits

Fruits are extremely rich in vitamins and are well liked by most toddlers. Bananas are rich in potassium, Vitamin B6 and magnesium, while mangoes and papayas both contain Vitamin C and A. Berries are also great for kids and can be made into healthy fruit shakes and smoothies. Fresh fruits can be a great snack for toddlers.

4. Whole Grains and Cereals

Whole grains are essential elements in a toddler's daily diet. For two-year-old tots, they need to consume at least 3 oz. of grains such as brown rice, oatmeal, wheat bread, pasta and whole grain cereals. Whole grains contain fiber to help prevent constipation.

5. Fish

Fish has low saturated fat content and very high in protein as well as Vitamin D and B. Fatty fishes such as mackerel and salmon contain Omega 3 essential fatty acids that are effective in boosting brainpower. However, there are certain fishes that contain contaminants (such as mercury and polychlorinated biphenyls) that should not be served to toddlers. Sharks, swordfish, king mackerel and tilefish are off the kid's menu.

Deciphering Food Labels

We all know that a boxed macaroni and cheese is not exactly what you can consider a nutritious meal for toddlers. But with our fast-paced lives, it becomes all too easy to choose prepackaged and processed food products over fresh and healthier choices. When shopping for food to feed your toddler and the rest of your family, here are some important things you need to watch out for when reading food labels:

Salt

Processed food products contain high amounts of salt since it presents an inexpensive option to add flavor as well as extend the shelf life of the product. Experts recommend no more than 2,300 mg of sodium per day. However one turkey sandwich that contains processed lunchmeat, condiments and cheese has about 1,300 mg of sodium, which is more than half of the recommended intake.

Sugar

A lot of kids today battle with obesity, mainly because of the high sugar content found in their food. Processed food products contain high amount of sugar and fructose corn syrup, which can trigger excessive weight gain. When reading food labels, sucrose, fruit juice concentrate, corn syrup, dextrose, glucose, maltose—all of these are different forms of sugar.

Percent Daily Values

The daily percent values are located on the right column in percentages. This indicates how much nutrient a person will derive from eating one serving of that food. So if a serving of a particular food product contains 18 % protein, then the said product will provide you 18% daily protein based on the 2,000 calories per day. Choose food products with nutrient value of 10 % to 19%, if the food only has 5% nutrient, it is considered low in nutrient content.

Saturated Fat and Trans Fat

The total amount of saturated fat appears right under the total fat content. The FDA requires food manufacturers to also indicate trans fat separately on the label. Both saturated fat and trans fat are considered "bad fats" mainly because they raise cholesterol levels. Saturated fats are mostly found in animal products such as ice cream, whole milk, cheese, butter and meat. On the other hand, trans fat is mostly in vegetable oil that have been treated or hydrogenated.

Avoiding Power Struggles at the Table

Feeding toddlers can be extremely frustrating. What should have been a pleasant mealtime can easily turn out to be a battle of wills and most often than not, parents end up losing the battle.

Power struggles at the table typically happen when parents force their toddler to eat. In order to avoid this, it is very important to understand toddler behavior. As we all know, most tiny tots are picky eaters, and they can be very particular on what they like and dislike. Additionally, you need to keep in mind that at this age, toddlers are slowly learning to exert control over their lives, eating is one of those few activities they will try to control.

Unlike babies or infants, toddlers are no longer at the stage of rapid growth, which means they become less hungry. This is why, feeding toddlers several snacks throughout the day in addition to regular meals is highly recommended. Here are some practical tips to help you regain a peaceful and enjoyable mealtime, while still giving your child the nutrients he needs:

1. Turn ordinarily meals into family time. Cultivate a fun and relaxed atmosphere and impose a "No TV" rule.

2. Feed your toddler the same type of food you feed to the rest of your family.

3. Do not force your toddler to eat. Issuing threats and punishments will only make him dislike and dread mealtimes.

4. Respect your toddler's food preference on what he likes and what he dislikes.

5. If he refuses to eat the main meal, offer another healthy alternative, like a sandwich or a cereal.

6. Make sure to cut your toddler's food into small bite size pieces.

7. Gently encourage your toddler to try out new food products.

8. Do not impose the clean your plate rule. When your toddler tells you he is full, do not force him to eat.

9. Offer your child small portions, like 1/3 or 1/4 of the usual adult portion. Give him lesser amount of food than what you think

he can consume and let him ask for extra servings.

10. Make desserts a part of your meals, and not as a form of reward.

Tips and Tricks on Feeding a Picky Eater

If toddlers were like fishes in the aquarium, feeding them would be a breeze. A fish doesn't have to be cajoled into eating dinner and a few sprinkles of flakes will be enthusiastically gobbled—no fuss, no crying and no whining. But the fact is, most toddlers are picky eaters. For any concerned parent, it can be an extremely annoying, frustrating and worrisome habit. So here are some great tips to help you feed your toddler without it turning into a battle royal:

1. Offer teeny-weeny servings. It can be quite difficult to encourage toddlers to try and taste something new. Instead of forcing it on them, try to offer small, non-threatening pieces, such as a cut of pea or a pink fleck of a salmon, or even a single grain of rice. Find humor on a simple activity and feed your child in a relaxed mood.

2. Get your kid to participate in meal preparation. By allowing your toddler to prepare the meal, they can look forward to tasting what they helped cooked.

3. Introduce your toddler to the different spices. Open the cabinet full of spices and let your child smell every single item, teaching them names for each one. It can also be a great idea to point out certain spices every time they may encounter it, such as oregano in pizza, cinnamon in French toasts, etc.

4. Feed them early. It is generally best to feed toddlers between 5 and 5:30 PM, or if they are extra hungry, even as early as 4:30 PM. Do not wait for everyone else to return from work to feed the child, when hunger is combined with tiredness, they can easily turn crabby.

5. Make toddler food plain and easy to eat. It is generally advisable to offer food separately, rather than offering them complex recipe mixed up in a casserole, and those with gravy and sauces.

Keeping Food Portions Under Control

While most toddlers are picky eaters, there are also a few who have impressive appetites. It is important for parents to know and understand portion sizes to best determine the amount of food to feed a toddler on a daily basis. If you allow your child to eat too much, it will eventually lead to unhealthy weight gain. Here is a basic guide to keep portion sizes in check:

Fruits and Vegetables

Fruits and vegetables should make up a major portion of your toddler's diet to provide sufficient amount of nutrients needed for growth and development. A toddler should have at least 2 to 3 tablespoons of vegetables per day, served in small bite size pieces. For fruits, one half of a fruit is considered a single serving. Give your child 4 to 5 servings of fruit per day.

Whole Grains

Bread, cereals and pasta supply your child fiber and protein. Food experts recommend three to four servings of grains on a daily basis. To give you an idea, a whole piece of bread or a cup of dry cereal makes a single serving.

Milk and Dairy

Milk is the most important component in a toddler's diet, as it is a major source of calcium and protein. For toddlers below 2 years old, serve full cream milk, since they need fat for brain development. However, for toddlers over 2 years of age, skimmed or low-fat milk is recommended to ensure they do not consume too much fat. A growing child needs to have 4 to 5 servings of milk each day, with half a cup making up a single serving.

Meat and Protein

Meat and beans are needed to provide your toddler sufficient amount of protein to grow muscles and bones. Food experts recommended serving food products that are low on saturated fat such as eggs, beans and lean white meat of chicken.

Toddlers require 2 servings of meat and protein-rich food per day. One single serving counts 1 to 2 oz. of lean meat, 2 tablespoons of peanut butter, 4 to 5 tablespoons of cooked beans, or 1 whole egg. If you plan to serve your child fish, make sure to check with your pediatrician first, since it is considered a high allergen food.

Skinny Sweets: Healthy Snacks for Toddlers

As your toddler grows older, it becomes doubly difficult to resist the lure of sweets. The great news is there are certain alternatives and approaches you can do to give your child sugary snacks, without causing damage to his teeth and health.

Sugary Sweets

1. Allocate a single day as a sweetie day. This way, your toddler will not constantly badger you for sweets.

2. Sweets should be eaten in one sitting rather than eating small portions all throughout the day. Make sure to ask your toddler to brush his teeth after eating sweets.

3. It is advisable to serve sweets after a meal. The amount of saliva in the mouth is increased when eating and it effectively neutralizes the ill effects of tooth-attacking acid.

4. Avoid giving sugar-rich products that stay in the mouth for prolonged period of time such as lollipops and candies.

5. Steer clear from sticky sweets such as toffee.

Sweet Drinks

1. Do not give acidic or fizzy, sugary drinks, especially in between meals.

2. Fruit juices are fine after every meal but should always be diluted. Make sure to

check out health drinks for kids for other forms of sugar such as lactose, glucose and fructose.

3. Try to offer water or milk as the primary choice. It will help if he constantly sees you drinking water during the day.

Skinny Sweets

1. Serve a bowl of washed grapes or carrot sticks straight from the fridge. Make sure to chop grapes in half to avoid choking.

2. Consider carrying a light snack with you when taking your toddler with you when grocery shopping. This way, you don't have to endure constant whining for sweets.

3. If your toddler seems to resist healthy snacks, allow him to choose fruits, cheese and vegetables. Kids are more interested in eating what they have personally chosen.

4. Make sure to offer food in variety of tastes and textures to keep your child

interested—crunch, smooth, cold, hot, sweet and sour.

5. Play with colors when choosing food and be creative in your presentation.

Here are some healthy snack ideas:

• Ants on a log—cut a celery stick and spread peanut butter on one side. Stick some raisins along the makeshift log so it will look like ants. Make sure your child is not allergic to peanut butter.

• Serve whole grain tortilla chips with salsa, veggies and shredded cheese. You can add guacamole as a dip.

• Make frozen fruit bars without adding any sugar, served with a glass of milk.

• Berries topped with a tiny amount of frozen yogurt.

• Dip a banana in yogurt, and then gently roll it in crushed cereal. Freeze it at least an hour before serving it as a frozen snack.

• Serve canned salmon mixed with a small amount of low-fat mayonnaise; you can use this mixture as a spread on whole grain crackers.

• Use a scoop of low fat frozen yogurt and sliced bananas as filling for a graham cracker.

• Serve baked pita chips, whole grain pretzels, soy crisps or rice cakes with a small slice of cheese.

Chapter 9: Lesson On Communicating With Your Kids

Effective communication is one of the secrets you should master if you want your kids to be happy, smart, and emotionally strong. You might think this is easy – after all, you talk to your children all the time – but being able to communicate effectively to kids takes more than just asking them questions and listening to their answers during your family dinners. Read the rest of this chapter to learn more about this parenting secret.

How to Engage in Positive Communication

Communicating positively with your kids will not only strengthen your relationship – it will also enable you to effectively teach them life lessons that you would want them to take to heart even when they are already on their own. Go through the points below to know more about how to engage in positive communication with your children.

Set the stage for open communication early on.

It will be easier for you to communicate effectively with your kids if you set the stage while they are still young. You can do this by letting them know through your words and actions that they are loved and accepted, and that they can talk to you openly and without fear of being criticized, mocked, or reprimanded. From the time that they learn how to talk, make sure that you pay attention and listen to them when they are saying something or asking questions. Also, pepper your conversations with them with positive messages. Doing so will encourage them to open up to you early on, and, provided that you are consistent with your parenting, will make it easier for them to talk to you when they are older. Positive messages, such as praising your kids when they do something nice, also reinforce good behavior.

Talk to them the right way.

As said earlier in this chapter, communicating with children does not only mean listening to their stories and talking to them whenever possible. Believe it or not, there is a right and wrong way of doing this. For instance, habitually interrupting your child when he is speaking may seem harmless to you – you're just commenting on what he's saying, after all – but it is actually something that child psychologists tell parents not to do.

If you are at a loss or are unsure as to whether you are encouraging effective communication with the way you talk to your kids, take note of the following tips:

Communicate at their level. When talking to your children – especially when answering their questions – try to make use of words that they will understand so as to avoid confusion and to be able to communicate with them effectively. Also, it's a good idea to literally go down to their level when engaging them in conversation: they are likely to feel intimidated if you tower over them when you are talking.

Schedule talks with them. Although it's good if you get to talk to your kids during sit-down meals and whenever you're at home, it's better if you set aside a specific time and day to engage in a lengthy, uninterrupted conversation with them. This will help you catch up with them and address any issues that may be bothering them. However, you need to be extra careful when following this tip; you wouldn't want to make them feel like the scheduled talk is a chore they need to do.

Replace the talk with an activity that the whole family can engage in and enjoy if you think there's no need to have an in-depth conversation with your kids at the moment.

Share your thoughts and feelings with them. Positive communication with your children is not just about letting them talk and listening attentively. On your end, you should also make it a point to share your ideas with them. This will show that you are interested in and are really listening to the conversation, which, in turn, encourages them even more to open up to you.

Strive to provide complete explanations... Answer your children's questions sufficiently to avoid confusion. There's no need for you to go into the details, especially if the issue is rather sensitive: just ensure that your explanation will not leave them wondering even more. Ask them if they have any more questions about the subject matter being discussed, and answer these briefly but accurately. On that note, you need to be careful with what you say when handling "grown-up" topics — filter your words and make them age-appropriate.

But make them brief. In as much as you want to explain something at length, refrain from doing so because this will make it more difficult for your kids to understand what you're saying. Just give them the gist of whatever it is you'd like to say, and then answer any follow-up questions they might have.

Don't hesitate to admit when you don't know something. It's better to tell your child that you don't know the answer to his question rather than make something up just to "save face". There's nothing wrong with letting your kids know that you don't always have the answer to their questions. In fact, you can make use of instances such as the one mentioned above to teach your child how to find the answer to a certain problem using the right tools and resources.

Really listen to them.

Effective communication also entails effective listening, which you can do by following these tips:

Ask questions. One of the best things you can do for your children to know that you are listening to them attentively is to ask questions that are relevant to what you are talking about. This is also a good way to show that you are interested in what they are saying. On that note, refrain from fielding questions that can be answered with a "yes" or "no". Instead, start your questions with "how" and/or the five Ws (who, what, when, where, and why) to encourage your kids to open up more.

Make eye contact. Whether you are talking or listening, it is important that you maintain eye contact with your kids during a conversation. This will let them know that they have your attention.

Refrain from interrupting. Interruptions can break a person's train of thought, which can be very frustrating. Thus, don't interrupt your child while he is speaking even if you have the urge to do so.

Focus on them during a conversation. Your children will get the impression that you are not interested in what they are saying if you're doing something else while they are talking to you. This will not only hurt their feelings, but also cause them to clam up in the long run. To encourage open communication with your kids, make it a point to eliminate any distractions during a conversation with them.

Chapter 10: Making A Statement Without 'Raising Your Voice'

If there is one thing that we have learned when it comes to dealing with our children, it is this: that it is very difficult to get them to comply with our wishes without raising our voices. Raising your voice is not the solution to getting your child to listen to you; it will only ensure that he or she rebels all the more in the future to come. Here are some ways to ensure that you keep a check on that 'voice' of yours and get the same things done effectively and in the calmest possible manner.

Use a positive expression.

When you are face to face with your child in an attempt to resolve conflict with them, you will find it will be most beneficial to you if you could put on your calmest face and add in a nice broad smile when you are trying to reason with them. You might be angry inside, but you should know you can never let that anger get the better of you because it won't solve anything. When you tell them things in a positive manner like 'There will be no TV after midnight' instead of merely yelling at them regarding the same, you will find that the results will be greatly beneficial to you when it comes to getting them to comply with your demands.

Have a sense of 'structure'.

This is by far the best thing you could possibly do when it comes to getting your kids to listen to you without having to senselessly yell at them. All you really need to do is establish a pre-defined schedule for them, one that can even be displayed someplace in the house where it can be prominently seen. For instance, in the point above I mentioned that you might one day find yourself yelling at your child to not watch television after dinner; when you have a pre-established schedule that maintains that they are not to do the same, it makes it easier to get your children to listen to the very same demands that might not work all that well were you to come up with them in an impromptu fashion and in the harshest manner possible.

Talk to your child about that 'yelling'.

In all probability the yelling duel between you and your child has been going on a lot longer than you could have ever imagined and it would be in your best interests (and in those of your child as well) to confront this very serious issue head on. You want to go up to your child one day and sit down with them, telling them that the two of you have been yelling at each other for far too long and this is something that you don't like. Tell your child that the next time you want them to listen to something you have to tell them, you are not going to yell at them. Instead you are going to tell them the very same thing one time and in a calm manner. Once you do that you can rest assured your child will look at you differently and will in all probability take what you are telling them in the future far more seriously.

Get out of an argument before it escalates.

No matter how hard you try, there will be times when your child yells at you and it is at times like these, more than ever, that you will find yourself losing your cool. It is important that when you are in a situation like this, you walk away without losing your temper. You could merely tell your child something like 'Okay, I'm not going to yell at you regarding this' and simply walk away. Then, when your child has cooled down sufficiently, they will see themselves the fallacy at having screamed at you, thus paving the way for them to see things in a different light altogether.

Learn to 'act' and not 'react'.

You might allow yourself to spiral out of control if you allow that anger that has been building inside you for a few moments to go unchecked. The worst possible thing about letting yourself get out of control and fly into a fit of rage is that you tend to 'react' and not 'act. Therefore, when your kid is running across the road you really want to 'act' and stop them from running instead of merely yelling at them not to. Recognizing anger early helps you 'act' and not merely 'react'.

Chapter 11: Newborn Babies

Now that you have brought your cute little baby home, what would be the next thing to do? Becoming a parent to a newborn baby can be a wee bit difficult, and at times, you might feel that you do not know what to do on certain occasions. Although taking care of a baby can be rewarding and fulfilling, you may find yourself not knowing what your baby needs when you hear him cry. The most basic things that you must do in order to keep your newborn baby happy are to give them enough rest, give them the right amount of care and sustenance, and obviously a huge amount of affection and love.

For your newborn babies to be strong and healthy, they need lots of resting time. This resting time can go for as long as sixteen hours every day, and once they turn three months old or more, they may be able to sleep for approximately six to eight hours every night. However, during the first few weeks of your newborn's life, they may sleep for two to three hours only at a time, and must be woken up by their parent if in case they were not fed for at least four hours.

There are instances when babies get confused with their nights and days, and some can become more active during the night while they sleep more during the course of the day. In the event that this happens, what you need to do is to simply limit the activity around them when they are awake. For instance, turn off the lights in their room and always talk in either low or hushed voices. Reorienting your baby's sleep cycles can take some time so be patient until you get the desired result.

In addition, when they sleep, always remember to change your baby's position in the bed occasionally to prevent soft spots, which are areas in the baby's face that appear when they spend an excessive amount of time sleeping with their head in just one position.

Breastfeeding

Another great thing you can do is to breastfeed your baby. It has already been proven by numerous studies that breastfeeding has a lot of positive effects on the health of your baby. The best time for you to begin breastfeeding is actually the moment after you first hold her after delivery.

To breastfeed, turn the body of your baby towards your direction so that you hold your baby's chest towards you. Using your nipple, touch your baby's upper lip and then pull her closer to your breast once she starts to open her mouth. After this, your baby should have locked her lips on your nipple, covering as much of your areola as possible. Once you get the hang of the process of placing your baby properly on your breast for breastfeeding, here are some other tips you may find useful:

If you have a difficult time getting your baby to breastfeed during your first few tries, do not tire out. Babies will naturally need to adapt first to the method of feeding that you would be implementing, and so it will take much of your time and patience. If you think that you cannot get your baby to breastfeed on your own, you can always ask for the help of someone who can help you, such as a lactation consultant or a nurse.

It is also important for you to take note that breastfeeding should not hurt you. If the baby's latching to your nipple hurts, you can break her suction by simply putting your pinkie between your breast and the gums of your baby repeatedly.

When you breastfeed, make sure that you eat a well-balanced and healthy diet. When you nurse your baby, you must be prepared for rapid instances of hunger, and you should also consider focusing on the increase in the amount of water you drink and the decrease in your caffeine and alcohol consumption. It is also important for you to be comfortable when you breastfeed since a single nursing session can take as long as forty minutes. When breastfeeding, choose a comfortable spot for you to sit in, and ensure that the place where you will be breastfeeding would give you enough back support.

During the first twenty-four hours of the birth of the baby, you should nurse her at an average of eight to twelve times. However, do not stick to a very strict feeding schedule. It is more suggested if you would simply feed your baby whenever she shows signs of being hungry, such as instances wherein your baby begins looking for your breast and when their mouth activity increases. On average, you must feed your baby once in every four hours, even if you need to wake your baby up gently in order for you to do so.

You will know that your baby receives a sufficient amount of food when you see that she makes an average of six to eight wet diapers every day. This should be accompanied by a consistent bowel movement, a steady gain of weight, and alertness when she is awake.

On the other hand, you can also formula feed your baby if that is more of your preference. Choosing formula feeding over breastfeeding is totally up to you, and to your judgment of whether the former would be much better than the latter. Although there are many studies that suggest breastfeeding is much better for your baby than formula feeding, you should also consider its impact on your health as well as the convenience of nursing, along with other significant factors.

Formula feeding makes it much easier for you to determine how much you are actually giving to your baby, and how much you need to cut down in the event that you realize that you are feeding your baby in excess. If you choose to feed babies through formula feeding, you have to remember the following:

Ensure that the bottles you will be using are properly sterilized.

You must follow the instructions that you will find on the label of the formula milk.

If there is formula milk left outside of the refrigerator for over an hour, or if your baby does not finish her formula milk, throw it away immediately.

Diapers

Another important thing that you should consider in taking care of your baby is changing diapers. For the first few years of your baby's life, you will need a lot of diapers and you need to be an expert really fast. Regardless of what method of diaper-changing you plan on taking, you need to be prepared to change your baby's diapers at an average of ten times every day. Here are the steps you should follow when you change your baby's diaper:

Make sure that everything you need is readily available. What you will need are fasteners (if you are the type of parent who uses cloth diapers), diapers, warm water on a container, diaper ointment, diaper wipes or cotton balls, and a clean washcloth

Take the dirty diaper off your baby. If the diaper is wet, position your baby on her back and take the diaper off, using the washcloth and the water to clean the genital area of your baby. For female babies, wipe them from front to back to make sure that you avoid UTIs. If you happen to see rashes forming, put ointment on them.

Open the new diaper up then gently and slowly slide it underneath your baby. As you do this, lift your baby's feet and legs gently. The diaper's front should be moved over the belly and between the legs of your baby. After that, bring around the adhesive strips so that the diaper is nicely fastened and secured.

In order for you to avoid diaper rash, make sure that you change the diaper of your baby as soon as she finishes with her bowel movement. Use soap and water to clean up your baby. It is also good if you would not put a diaper on your baby right away so that her bottom would be able to air out for quite a bit.

Baby Baths

When it comes to bathing your baby, it is important that you know how to do it properly in order to avoid accidents. Bathing babies can be easy and fun for both you and the baby. In the first week of the baby's life, make sure that you give her a nice sponge bath. When the umbilical cord falls off on its own, you can begin regularly bathing your baby in as much as twice or thrice every week.

In order for you to bath your baby in the right way, you will need supplies, which include soap, towels, and a clean diaper.

All of these need to be prepared in advance so that your baby would not fuss around. Before you start with the bath, you should also fill up your baby's tub with at least three inches of warm water.

If you feel uncertain about bathing your baby alone, you can ask for someone's help to assist you. This is something that you might feel during the first time you are actually going to give your baby a bath, that is why it is important for you to feel that it is okay to seek help. You can get either your partner or a particular family member involved, so that one of you can hold the baby and the other would bathe her.

Carefully take your baby's clothing off. After that, with the feet first, slip your baby carefully into the tub. Use one of your hands as a support for the neck and hands of your baby. Pour cupfuls of warm water in the bath so that your baby would not be cold.

Once the baby is in the bathtub, use a mild soap to clean your baby. Use it only sparingly so that you do not get any into the eyes of your baby. When washing your baby, use either your hands or a washcloth. Wash your baby beginning from the top to the bottom, and then from the front to the back. Make sure that you manage to clean your body's scalp, hair, body, and genitals. Also, make sure that you get to clean up any accumulated dried mucus on your baby's face.

Again, using cupfuls of water, rinse your baby. Using the washcloth, wipe your baby until she is completely clean. Afterwards, lift your baby gently from the tub, with one hand supporting her head and neck. Take extra care when lifting your baby since their skin may tend to become slippery.

Pat your baby dry and then put her in a hooded towel. Then, put a dress and a diaper on your baby, then kiss her so that she can associate bath time with positive emotions.

It is also important to keep your baby physically and emotionally healthy. Since babies spend a lot of time laying on their backs, it is important for you to give them enough time to stay on their tummies. This will help them develop the strength of their head, arms, and neck. There are doctors who suggest that babies should get at least fifteen to twenty minutes of being on their tummies every day, although there are others who say that you should put your babies on their tummies for approximately five minutes on different parts of the day as your babies develop.

Tummy time can begin as soon as the umbilical cord falls off, which is roughly about a week after birth. There are going to be times when this would become difficult, with the baby resisting to lay on their tummies, but there are things you can do to encourage them. In order to make their time on their tummies fun, you can position yourself at level with your baby. You can then play around with your baby while you tickle her and while you are maintaining eye contact.

Chapter 12: How Dads Can Usurp The Power Of Peer-Pressure?

How can one explain the attainment of good upbringing, despite imperfections of the parents? Simply because, the kids and the parents, are fallible human beings. Even at that, I didn't set out to bring up morons or robots as kids, but to guide them to seek wisdom and use it in their lives.

It was by constant dialogue, from their cradle and showing demonstrable discipline from my end. I had to be available once I had the opportunity.I could not leave the task only to their mum. I had a responsibility. I brought it the innocent kids to my world. I should be ready for it.
I should nurture these seeds to become big trees, that can serve as a shade to itself and while others go under its canopy, to enjoy its coolness..

If they were girls, maybe my wife could have done it much better, alone. But boys always need a responsible male or father figure. Such persons could be a honest but committed uncle, family-friend of clean character. The job is to assist a boy-child, to engage our world full of roving wolves with selfish agenda. And of course a parent must behave decently and aim to usurp the so-called role of peer pressure.

A good upbringing can also be a source of peer-pressure. Why not? It doesn't have to be bad character as popularized. In-fact, if our kids are told that they are special (I told mine) they could be a source of influence too. They could be the source of peer-pressure amongst their friends. Why should people of shady or bad character influence school mates? I told them it was about self-esteem, conviction and confidence. It was about leadership, which comes with courage while they assess different scenarios around them. An individual could choose to influence even if his position wasn't popular. I explained to them that this mindset was liberating eventually. And if laced with good conscience and behavior they could influence others. But it won't be easy and they should be ready for that challenge.

Talking about influence, Oh, that reminds me of the advent of the internet, which got everybody excited, including me. So how did I take my boys through the new experience at their early teenage years? I remember in the year 2002, mind you they were brought up in Africa. I discovered the excitement amongst young people about the Internet and the huge voyeuristic appeal it had on young people. I knew it was a tool of dual personality; for good and the bad. Most people patronized the public cybercafe. That was the initial set up, to surf. Today the ubiquitous cell phones have put the experience, at everyone's finger tips with more intimate privacy.

And so, what did I do? I didn't let them take a plunge without sharing a few words with them. I made them to note that this new exciting tool could be used for good or bad. I was the first person to give them the money to pay for their first one hour, of browsing time. I advised they could visit sites that would be useful to them or other naughty sites that will not add useful information to their existence. I gave them the opinion that at their age some young folks were already using the internet positively, while others used them for nefarious activities. The choice was theirs. I let them go since. I told them, good causes were quite difficult to push further in today's culture that people would laugh at you. Good people still have their place under the sun, even while it is tough to maintain integrity. . And I would give practical examples all over the world to buttress my point.

This kind of Socratic dialogues went on, even when I visited them in the boarding school on their monthly visiting day, with my wife. A short discussion always came up before we say bye. My wife did what I couldn't do as a man. On such visits, she came with fresh school uniforms and clothes they would wear. Their shoes. Their school bags. The groceries for their side locker in the boarding schools, she took care of them.

During school vacations, when they are at home, on some Saturday mornings and other occasions, we talked. I could lap into what the media - including the online social media were insinuating, to trigger off discussions. The three of us could be getting ready for the bath, with tooth-brushes in our hands, either caught standing or sitting. I will iron out some issues, values and explain certain things. Before we knew it, I had taken one hour or so of their time. When I suspected I was becoming boring or tired myself, I wrapped up. It used to be a monologue but now I listen more when they engage me on varied issues. I was discussing with a friend, few years back and was surprised he used the same approach of connecting with his twin boys and another son. They came out to be well behaved young men, despite the fact that, they reside in a seedy part of the city. When the sudden Socratic dialogue ensued, his wife would let "the men of the house" be, while she kept herself occupied in the distance. My wife still does same.

Equally, when my boys were in the kitchen, with their mum and I noticed that they were engrossed in some talks, I knew it was wise for me to keep away. Whatever knowledge they were grabbing from their mum, makes for a balanced outlook of the children. Wise parents should recognize and respect the importance of each loving parent or guardian.

When A Father Is Away From Home
Parenting by dads might appear like a mirage and so challenging, if your job involves regular trips away from home, to earn a living. The trick is to put the family in your schedule, as much as you can. Technology makes it easy these days, for human interaction. But it may not replace the needed minimal physical interaction required to look after your boys. When you come home, reappraise and continue from where you stopped the last time. Assist your partner or wife as she can't do it alone!

I was always conscious of that. This means whenever I saw my kids, I wanted to know what had transpired, when I was not available.

At times, one couldn't find answers to some aspects of parenting but you can always ask friends or those much older in the affairs of taking care of kids. For those who have well spaced kids, there comes a time, when the well brought-up senior kid would be in a position to guide the younger ones, in the absence of the parents.

The Positive Fallouts

I told myself that my wife and I would strive to have a piece of mind, as we get older. And I knew bad kids could be a pain in the neck. And I wanted the kids to be helped for their own good too. Then I would have done my bit with the hope that my efforts would yield fruit. These were my thoughts at their infancy.

I married young and my first son came when I was about 27 years of age. The second came, when I was at about 30. I was a young working professional like my wife, almost fresh from the university. The unexpected pregnancy quickened the wedlock.

That did not prevent me from acquiring additional skills while I pursued my executive MBA classes as a married man with an infant. My wife did not secure a job quickly until a few months after. I earned far more than her and we both took care of the family. Many years after, fate reversed the role of the bread-winner. She found herself in the role. We had our short altercations. It was stressful for me and her.

But I pulled through and bounced back to earning, deservedly today. I believe both of us learnt quite some lessons. The children watched and understood the trial period. We informed them. Today, everybody is at peace and strong, to tame the tidal wave of unexpected uncertainties.

A blessing in disguise for the young adult-kids, about life and strength for we, the parents, to be proactive against possible re-occurence of those strenuous years.

Twenty eight years down the line as I pen this, the first young man had traversed different parts of Europe, while doing his succesful Masters degree in Germany. We never visited him once or had cause to fear of any misbehavior. The younger brother can hold his own today at his place of work as a varsity graduate, with multiple skills.

It has not been a smooth sailing relationship, a few times; they have disagreed with my views. I have allowed with reasons. My wife and I are happy with them. And they have equally shown so much palpable love, in return to us - and to other people, mindful of the trickery of the world and its funny people.

Showing Examples As A Dad

At times as men, we want to appear to be of good behavior to our children. Some of us do the opposite outside the family stead. That's ok. We should be mindful that boys tend to ape their fathers, in action but would rather divulge their innermost secrets to their mum. So fathers; mind that naughty behavior of yours and manage it. When we are with our friends, we can let loose of our naughtiness. I understand. Let's protect our adult secrets and cut them off if possible. In bringing up my boys, I had had cause to smoke cigarette on a few occasion, only known to my wife as a truncated adventure. But I won't even regard myself as a smoker. If I recall, the number of sticks I might have taken, since my adulthood, possibly may not be up to two packs. And the last single stick, maybe four years ago. Just being curiosity. So we adults get tempted too, till we leave this earthly space at the appointed time. But I do take my occasional one bottle of beer once in a while, which I could share with my first adult son when I am at home. My second son doesnt' like alcohol. And I seldom drink.

Chapter 13: Booby Traps To Avoid

Trips, Slips and Falls

In life in general there are many booby traps that people can fall into that will change their lives (almost) forever. That is one of the reasons God gave children parents. It's a parent's job to guide their offspring through the many minefields the child will inevitably encounter along the road to adulthood.

Since the parent has already walked the road to adulthood, they are well aware of possible hazards the average teenager (in any given culture) may face.

Usually the parent is ready and willing to warn their youngster of impending pitfalls; however, some parents may need to hone their communication skills in order to be able to convey such experiences to their child effectively.

Therefore, this chapter is more about coaching the parent in how to address some of the many issues that could throw their teenager off course. The problem is rarely that parents don't know the names of the obstacles their youngster will encounter; the problem is more that parents are not always equipped to successfully communicate their wisdom to their teen.

Getting Acquainted

As a rule, parents feel they know their child better than anyone else could possibly know them. In my opinion, parents are rightly offended when counselors or well meaning outsiders start trying to tell the parent who their child is. I'm highly offended when outsiders start trying to tell a child they are the child's "friend". Of course, not always, but most often the child is better served if outsiders point the child toward their parent – who REALLY is their highly invested friend!

With that said, let me ask you this. Does your teenager know who he is? Does he feel lost, or does he have a firm grip on what his purpose in life is and what direction he wants to take once he reaches adulthood? If your teen has not come to terms with who he is and what his purpose in life is, then he will likely be a lot more vulnerable to falling into the many negative traps he encounters along the road to adulthood.

Helping your teenager solidify his character by supporting his goals to become a person with integrity will pay big dividends in the long run for both of you, the parent and the child. It's essential that teenagers have had a solid foundation of knowing how to make good choices and then having the conviction to stand by the choice they made.

Parents can help their child develop a sense of right and wrong, as well as a sense of purpose and direction by not only making sure your child is exposed to healthy groups (such as scouting and extracurricular opportunities at school), but by setting the example of getting involved in community service and other purpose driven activities as well.

Parents who set a good example for their child early by teaching how to resolve conflicts calmly and skillfully will reap the benefit during the teen years. Such training helps children learn how to handle their own anger and frustrations, without using violence, further down the road.

Additionally, parents can lay the foundation of good, moral character by living a life that doesn't always choose the easy road. Make sure your teenager sees you apologize for a mistake, or being a person who keeps your word, for instance. The old saying, "character is better caught than taught" is still true today. The stronger your teens character the less likely they will fall into a social trap that could alter their life forever.

Dealing With Missed Steps

There was only one perfect person – and they killed him, so that means the rest of us will have to learn to deal with our shortcomings as we move through life. My point is, we mere mortals are only human and that means we all make mistakes. Learning to take the proper steps to get past our offences with the least amount of collateral damage is not a science – it's an art.

A major tool a parent can use to help their teen stay on course is to make sure the teenager has set both long and short-term goals for himself.

Parents can sit down with their teen and LISTEN to the aspirations their child has for the future.

This is not a place for the parent to try to inject his or her own opinions.

The parent needs to go mute and try to hear their child's heart in what they desire for their future. Parents need to be open to a broad range of acceptable and less acceptable goal setting at this point. The whole point of this interaction is to determine if your child has thought about their future in a serious way or not.

Have your child write out (on paper) their long-term goals, and then have them identify their short-term goals. It's best if parents do this exercise as early in the teen years as possible. This tool alone can be an invaluable help to a parent who wants to keep their child on track during their trip from childhood to adulthood.

Once you have the child's goals in writing it will give you a focal point in a wide variety of situations. For example, if your child's grades start to drop you can revisit the goals document and discuss what steps need to be taken to get back on track.

If your teenager is struggling in school – either academically or socially – try to calmly get to the bottom of the problem. For teenagers, school is a vital part of their lives. Their success in high school often sets the direction they will head into as adults. Therefore, don't hesitate to invest time and money into your teenager's high school career.

Chapter 14: Raising An Optimistic Child

A child who is raised in a healthy environment will grow up a happy person. His positive experiences will help him deal efficiently and effectively with the roadblocks and adversities of life. You have a big role in nurturing optimism in your child.

Here are some tips on how to do it.

Show a positive example to your child. While growing up, he needs to see that his parents display positive outlook in life. It will not help if your child hears you utter curses from time to time. Your child will more likely mimic your habits and behaviors so make sure you exhibit traits that will develop his well-being in a positive way.

Allow your child to succeed. You may do this while helping him explore his creative mind. Let him create short-time goals and give him time to achieve them. Examples of children's short-time goals are drawing one picture, building a community (using toys such as LEGO), and finishing a book. In addition to that, you may also offer him some activities around the house and appreciate his efforts when he's done.

Focus on his efforts. You can celebrate an achievement for one day. But don't get too attached with what your child has achieved instead appreciate his efforts in sticking with his task and finishing it. Recognize his ability to get through the tough process and being able to overcome the obstacles until he accomplished his goal. This is the best way for him to learn that success comes from hard work.

Look forward to your child's future success. Examine the traits your child exhibited while trying to achieve his goals. Make him aware of these traits and help him realize how much you admire him for all those traits.

Allow him to develop his sense of humor. One of the best ways to keep an optimistic perspective in life is by laughing at your own mistakes. If you can laugh at your mistakes, it will be easier for you to find ways to correct them. You don't get frustrated instead you are able to deal with it calmly and patiently.

Allow your child to grow at his own pace. Don't force him into the adult world. As much as possible, don't expose him to the harsh and sad realities of adulthood.

Help your child see his mistakes as opportunities to do better next time. Don't blame him when something went wrong. Instead, allow him to examine his mistakes and help him find ways to improve.

Help your child see the brighter side of a bad day. Let him see the good and bad in every situation then help him look for the silver linings in circumstances that did not turn out positively.

Don't use negative labels when addressing your child's shortcomings. Some parents are fond of calling their children with unbecoming labels such as whiner or immature. These labels could become permanent identities. If you are doing this then drop it now to avoid perpetuating the behaviors you don't want your child to develop.

Teach your child to think positively. Help him learn how to approach problems with a positive point of view.

Optimists do better in school and work because they are less likely to experience depression. If your child develops a positive attitude in his early life, he will become more resilient as an adult. He will enjoy a happier life with less stress and conflicts.

Chapter 15: Backtalk

You're cooking dinner when you ask your toddler to clear all of his coloring stuff off of the table so the family can sit together. Suddenly, out of nowhere, he screams, "No!" You might stand there stunned, looking at this little creature you created wondering where this attitude has come from or you might get angry and fly off of the handle refusing to be disrespected by a child.

You may find yourself wondering if this means that you are going to have to suffer through years of back talk and sassing as you do your best to raise a proper human being. You may not be in for years of back talk and sassing as it turns out.

The reason that toddlers back talk is the same as why they throw tantrums and why they become aggressive. Toddlers that back talk are simply trying to express their emotions, whether it be anger, frustration, fear, jealousy or hurt. They may back talk because they are tired or hungry, because they are in a situation that they are not used to or because they are simply seeing how much they can get away with.

Of course, no matter how great of a parent you are, it can be hard at times to not respond to back talk with our own anger or hurt feelings, but it is important that you do not do this.

What you should do, however, is to find out what it is that is upsetting your toddler and then teach your toddler the appropriate way to express themselves. You need to remember that it is not your child's feelings or emotions that are the problem. The problem is how your child is expressing their feelings or emotions.

What can a parent of a toddler do about back talk? The first thing that you as a parent have to do when your toddler begins back talking is to determine if the back talk is preventable. There are situations that you will find as you are raising a toddler where back talk seems almost inevitable. For example, if you tell your child to clean up their toys when they are in the middle of playing, chances are that there is going to be some back talk. However, there are steps that you can take, which will prevent a lot of this back talking. In this situation, you could let your child know that they have five minutes to finish up playing and then they will need to move on to the next task of their day whether that is meal time, nap time, bath time or whatever else.

Another situation that you might encounter is that the child will not stay in their bed. Often, you will find that the child says he hates his blanket, his bed is stupid, or he hates his room. If you spend a few minutes talking to your child, you might find that the child is actually afraid. There could be a multitude of reasons that your child is afraid to sleep in their bed, but there is one thing that usually deals with this issue, and it is the light. Get the toddler a night light or allow them to keep a flashlight under their pillow so they can flick it on when they see a shadow move across the wall. This will ensure that they know they are safe and that there is nothing in the room that is going to get them.

Make sure that you are choosing your battles wisely. When a parent lays out a child's clothes for them, especially a toddler, chances are the toddler is going to have something to say about the choice of clothing. Often, this can lead to an all-out fight between the toddler and the parent, but is it really worth it? If the child does not like the shirt that you have laid out for him or her, let the child know that they can choose a different shirt, but that it is not okay for them to speak to you disrespectfully or to be mean to you. There is no reason to get into an argument over what shirt will be worn to the grocery store.

Find out where the behavior is coming from. Many times, we do not realize what our children may be exposed to. One thing that I have learned through years of parenting is that some of the 'kids' television shows should not really be watched by kids, especially toddlers. Many shows depict a smart mouthed child as funny or cute, and your child may be learning this behavior by watching these types of television shows. Keep an eye out for influences, even if it is your child's cousin that is displaying this type of behavior, nip it in the bud because your child is going to pick up on that. You will learn so much more about what I am talking about when your sweet toddler starts school, and suddenly, you will have no idea who the child is anymore. The point is, there are influences everywhere, and they can change the way that your child behaves.

Make sure that your child knows what the rules are ahead of time. If you do not want your child saying, "That looks nasty," or "I'm not eating that," at the dinner table, you need to ensure that the child knows this is a rule. If the child does not know something is a rule, you cannot expect them to follow it.

You need to make sure that your expectations are clear and that when the child fails to meet these expectations, you are simply going to remind him or her that we do not speak that way when we are... (E.g. at the dinner table).

Sometimes we need to remind our toddler that while we love to hear what they think about the world, other people may not be as happy to do so. The cashier at the grocery store does not need to be told that she has a big butt, and grandma does not need to know that her pie is not as good as mommy's. This is where we begin teaching our child about how they should behave in public but trust me, they are going to embarrass you at least a few times, and you should be ready to apologize and remind your child in front of the person that they are not to speak to people that way.

Stay calm when your child starts back talking. Of course, many parents go with the knee-jerk response of, "Don't you talk to me like that," or some version of that. They get angry and feel disrespected, but a better way to handle the situation would be to tell the child that you think they can come up with a nicer way of saying whatever it is that they have said to you, and do not respond to them until they change what they have said.

Make sure that the child understands that you care about the way they are feeling and understand that they are upset. Many parents forget to let the child know that what they are feeling is completely normal, but instead jump right to yelling at the child or disciplining him or her for their behavior. If your toddler feels as if you do not understand how they are feeling, chances are they are going to turn up the back talking and aggressive behaviors until you acknowledge what they are feeling.

One good way to do this is to help them put words to their feelings. Ask the child if he/she is angry and find out what upset him/her. Ask if they are tired and so on, making sure that the child knows that you understand what they are going through. Try to get past the child's tone of voice and understand what message he or she is trying to send you.

Allow your toddler to have some choices. I spoke earlier about how toddlers were starting to gain their independence, and as much as we may not like it, they do want to start making some of their own choices. When a toddler feels like he or she has made a choice on their own, they are less likely to back talk and misbehave.

Of course, you want to give the child limited choices, e.g. "Do you want to wear the red or the blue shirt?" "Do you want pasta or rice?" and so on. Only let the child pick from two or three things. Otherwise, the child will become overwhelmed, and you will end up with a bunch of back talk and possibly a tantrum on your hands.

Stop asking, "Okay?" When you put the word "okay" at the end of a sentence, you are literally asking the toddler for permission to move on to the next task. For example, "Bath time, okay?" This makes the toddler feel as if they have a choice in the matter, but what happens when they say no? Generally, what happens is that the parent gets upset and tells the child they said it was bath time when in reality they asked if it was bath time. This can cause the toddler to become upset and cause back talking as well as aggressive behaviors. Simply tell the child what you expect. "Bath time is in five minutes," letting the child know that they will be transitioning from whatever activity they are doing to bath time, and they need to mentally prepare themselves for that. When you do this, you will find that there is much less back talk.

Finally, it is important for you not to try and bribe the child. "If you put on your coat without throwing a fit, I will buy you ice cream." No. This is simply bribing the child to do what you want them to do, and it is not teaching them anything except that they do not have to do what you ask unless you offer them a reward for doing so.

If you want to surprise your child with ice cream, that is fine, tell him or her that they are receiving it because they have been so well-behaved but don't use it as a tool to get them to behave.

Back talking can be frustrating for many parents, but when you really take the time to get to the bottom of it, you will quickly begin to understand what is upsetting your child, and back talking will be a thing of the past.

Chapter 16: Be The Role Model & Instill Good Manners

A child at their early life stages is very easily influenced by the surrounding medium. They tend to imitate, copy and pursue what the surrounding adults (and other children) do, say and practise. As a parent, it is your precious inevitable responsibility to be the one whom your child can mimic and learn from widely, regularly and for the long run. As a father, you should represent the ideal (or at least acceptable) decent honourable role model of what a man should be like. As a mother, you should in turn represent an honourable and beautiful image of a good woman and lady. Do not act improperly towards each other and towards other people, and then complain about your children misbehaving repeatedly. It is in most cases attributed to your own misbehaviours, having been copied and mimicked by them.

Generally speaking, being a good role model for your child, regardless of you being the mum or dad, can comprise a lot of pleasant activities and deeds demonstrated by you. To name a few:

Demonstration of love, respect and appreciation between spouses. The more genuine and sincere this demonstration is, the more beautiful it would seem and the more positive vibes would be emitted. Well, you should as spouses be acting as such towards each other, regardless of children being present or not! Avoidance of using coarse language and inappropriate phrases, even within jokes. Avoidance of demonstrating impoliteness and a troublemaking attitude while outdoors, usually expressed by coarse language with people, quarrelling, using inappropriate phrases, misbehaving in public, raising your voice, savage uncivilised acting, sexual and verbal harassment of people and women, and so many more.

Following the etiquettes while outdoors: throwing litter in their specified baskets, behaving in public transport (sitting quietly, giving the seat to people in need like the elderly, reading a book,…), crossing the street when the pedestrian sign indicates the time to do so, speaking with a low-pitch voice in public places like restaurants and shops, decently and politely negotiating and conversing with people even in the case of a trouble – you surely wouldn't like your kid to grow into a troublemaking intolerable bully, not staring at people aimlessly nor approaching them without their permission – you as well don't wish your kid to become a harasser, do you?

Your intellect, perspectives and views of life can be directly and indirectly instilled in your kid's brain and contribute in the long run to formulating the individual they're going to be like in years. You may be adopting any creed and any category of life perspectives: you may be conservative, liberal, secular, politically radical, religiously radical, moderately religious, non-religious, environment-friendly, vegan, vegetarian, fanatic, patriotic, feminist, misogynist, LGBT supportive or opponent, animal rights supportive, racist, anti-racist,… you can be any of those and you are fully entitled to that, but remember that at least a minimal proportion of what you adopt would almost inevitably get to the intellect of your child, and may be either absorbed and accepted by their intellect, or rejected and replaced with some other perspective that is more suitable.

Manners to be instilled in your kid are a plenty, many of which can be automatically and passively transferred to them through witnessing you implementing these manners in real-life situations. To name only a few of these manners – which are certainly supposed to be good! – we have kindness, respecting elder people, politeness, avoidance of aggression and offence of others, self-confidence, capability to stand for oneself (self-defence) when necessary but without offending others nor hurting them, using polite expressions depending on situations, gratefulness, appreciation and satisfaction with what they have, respecting people regardless of their ethnicity, religion, nationality, skin colour, social class or other factors that separate people rather than unite them. There is also expressing apology when needed – ONLY when needed; your child is not supposed to plead guilty nor apologise all the time, and the responsibility lies upon you here to properly instruct them to recognise when they should acknowledge their mistakes and when they should defend themselves and refuse to apologise uselessly. Another good manner is forgiveness, which also needs to be moderated by you – instruct your child to recognise when it becomes not preferred to forgive, especially when it is expressed to the same person who appears to be persisting in their wrongdoings rather than rectifying them and feeling remorseful. Teaching manners therefore should be balanced: ingrain good manners but without exaggeration to the extent of rendering your child's personality fragile and insecure. Simultaneously, instruct about bad manners and their harms, encourage towards avoiding them, and teach how to manifest strength and a good level of self-esteem away from unpleasant mannerism.

Chapter 17: Managing Finances

In the first chapter of this book we briefly touched on trusting your teenager with money for shopping. Some teenagers can be flippant when it comes to their finances. Mario Balotelli, the Italian football player, famously took $50 that he was given to buy groceries and returned with a second hand dirt bike that he purchased from a stranger on the street. Sometimes there does not seem to be an rhyme or reason to our children's spending habits, but when they are living at home there is really not too much for them to worry about. Once they are out in the world on their own it is a completely different story.

Teaching your children how to be responsible through managing their own finances can be one of the best things you will ever teach them. Money plays a central role in determining the type of life that people live. So let's go through some lessons that you can teach your teenager now about managing their finances in a smart way.

Lesson #13: Credit Management

Credit cards need to be properly managed as they can quickly rack up interest and fees that your child may not be able to pay back. Banks will give away credit cards with proof of seemingly any amount of income. Initially the card limit will be set relatively low, but once your child gains a credit score by repaying the amounts spent on the card for a few consecutive months that limit will be approved to increase.

My children both qualified for credit cards at the age of 15. They were working at part time jobs earning roughly $200 per week. This allowed them a max credit limit of $500. After 6 months of having his credit card my son got a letter from the bank informing him that his credit limit had been approved to increase to $2,000 if he so wished. That is 10 weeks wages for a 15 year old! If he had taken it it could have afforded him all kinds of things that he wanted to buy - only to then start charging him 18% interest on anything he could not repay after 55 days.

Luckily he did not increase the card and I was able to explain the correct usage of a credit card. Before your child gets out to start a life of his/her own, it is important that you do the same for them. They should know how a credit card works and the consequences for using it incorrectly before going out in the world and spending at will.

Lessons in credit cards

How a credit card works. Repayment dates, interest rates, monthly charges, and how to access information online.

Note: You are normally given this information when signing up for a credit card and could find it on your specific bank's website. Failing this please see:

The importance of spending within certain limits to avoid being trapped in credit card debt. If you cannot afford to make repayments by the end of the month then do not buy it.

Help them to cue monthly credit card payments. In as much as this may seem simple and obvious to you, it may sound like rocket science to them. Whether it is an automatic payment, a mark on the calendar, or an alarm on their phone does not matter, you need to instill in them an urgency to meet repayments on time. You don't want them to be missing paying credit card payments resulting to different penalties that could even damage their credit score!

Why you need to keep your credit card information private. Don't just assume that they know! This means alerting your child to fraudulent emails and sites that may steal personal information and teaching them how to stay safe from identify theft. For example if a Nigerian prince is asking for your bank details so he can transfer you money and get into the country you should recognize it as a scam and delete it.

Train your kids about the importance of changing credit card PIN to something they can remember but that is hard for anyone to guess. Try to instill in them the need to be responsible and careful in what they do in order to keep their credit card information safe.

Key Takeaways

In the world that we live in credit is easy to come by. Your child will no doubt be exposed to it one way or another. It is much better for you as a parent to take the time while your teenager is still living at home to educate them on how and why to use a credit card. It can save them a potentially very hard and expensive lesson by learning it in theory from you rather than in practice by going out and making mistakes themselves.

Lesson #14: Saving for a rainy day

Teaching kids the importance of setting aside money for a rainy day fund is always a good idea. It promotes the concept of living below your means and can teach your child how to reach goals through saving. Here is how I taught my children the importance of savings.

Lessons on savings

Firstly it is important to have a goal.

A rainy day fund for an adult it a completely different beast than for a teenager. If you want to convince them that saving is a good idea, put up a fun target to aim for. I used a family vacation as this target and told my oldest that we were planning it but could no longer afford to take him as well. He was 17 and working part time and spending all of his money on himself every time he received his paycheck. I gave him a few months warning and worked out with him that if he put 10% of his earnings every week into a savings account that we created that he would be able to afford to come on the trip and that we would pay for all of the hotels and food when we got there. Of course he didn't want to organize anything on his own so was motivated to achieve this goal and come along for a holiday.

You can do similar things with your children even if they are much older. If you have been paying for something and they expect you to continue then you have a bargaining chip to hold over them to encourage this change in spending.

Create an automatic payment to a locked savings account

My daughter who is now 24 is the type of person who easily bends and breaks when trying to save. She will see something that she simply must have, and knowing that it ruins a savings plan to reach a goal she wants to achieve she will buy the item. For some people it is hard to differentiate between needs and wants such as this. But what we came up with to help her save was an automatic payment out of her account on the day she gets paid. 10% of her income goes straight to a savings account that has to be cosigned by both my daughter and my husband to access it. This creates a failsafe that she needs to stick to her savings plans moving forward.

Rewarding yourself for progress is necessary

Have you ever been saving towards a large goal that just felt constantly out of reach? I definitely have. Saving for a deposit on a house seemed like we were living on a miniscule income for years. At times it was terrible - I wanted to go out and buy something nice but didn't want to ruin the savings plan.

It is important to know yourself and to teach your kids that rewarding yourself for small wins when working towards a big goal is essential. Rewards are the motivational force that keep us going. So if you are teaching your kids to save 10% of their income per month, make sure that at the end of the month they have $50 to set aside to go and spend on themselves. A nice dinner, a piece of clothing, a night at the movies - it doesn't matter. Just go out and enjoy the fact that you achieved your goal. Then the next day start working towards the next one.

Key Takeaways

Teaching your teenager how to save using these very simple steps can have a huge impact on the rest of their life. If your children can get in the habit of living below their means then they can put themselves in a position to accumulate savings to be put towards property, investments, or travel and holidays.

Another great benefit of having an emergency fund is that it can cover the medical costs for minor accidents and any expenses that may come their way. Life is full of little annoying surprises that require forking out money as I am sure you are well aware if you are reading this. Things like dentist visits, pet surgery, or home repairs and maintenance are all things that having a rainy day fund could be put to use paying for. This work beautifully for you as a parent as your teenager would no doubt ask you for money to cover such incidents if they did not have savings to cover it.

Lesson #15: How to manage debts

There is smart debt and bad debt in this life. Financing the purchase of assets that can generate an income or a profit such as buying and house, a business, or college education can be considered smart debt. Borrowing money can help your child to purchase things that they would not have otherwise been able to afford. It is however important to teach your kids how to manage debts, and how to know when to stop borrowing.

Steps to take to teach children how to manage debts

Work out how much your teen can afford to borrow

You might not be a financial advisor that feels comfortable giving advice on investments and subsequent repayments, but you can refer your teen to get the correct advice online. 'Sorted' is a website created by the NZ government to help people accurately calculate debt repayment schedules. It works by entering in incomes and expenditures and working out exactly how much they can afford in repayments and therefore how much they should borrow.

Work out what is smart debt and what is not.

Once again I would recommend going to 'Sorted' for this. They break down credit card, personal loan, and hire purchase debt structures and give you calculators to work out the exact cost to you of purchasing something from savings or by borrowing.

Recently I read about a 24 year old girl who had borrowed $3,000 as a personal loan to go on holiday. When she got back from the holiday she could not meet the repayments as she had some other pressing bills so she took out a second loan to pay off the repayments from the first. It has now been 14 months and her $3,000 debt has increased to $32,000 with a string of personal loan companies and loan sharks. Her whole family was pitching in to help make repayments as the interest was multiplying the debt at an alarming rate that she would never be able to afford.

This is an extreme example, but by no means is it a one off case. People find themselves in financial trouble due to over stretching their financial capability to repay the debt. By teaching your child to be smart about borrowing hopefully they will be able to avoid such circumstances.

Key Takeaways

If you do not teach your teen lessons in managing debt they can quickly find themselves in financial trouble. You do not need to be an expert to give them this advice, you just need to set them on the right path.

Teach your teenager how to recognize what is smart debt and what is not, and how to work out what they can afford in repayments. It could make the difference between drowning in debt and working towards financial security. As well as avoiding penalties your teachings have the added advantage of helping your child's credit rating. Repaying a debt successfully boosts their credit ratings which means that they can apply for another loan in the future at a lower interest rate.

Chapter 18: Common Behavior Concerns

As they grow, all children are likely to go through challenging situations that cause worrisome thoughts. The role of parents is not necessarily to eliminate anxiety but to help control it. Prothero, a psychologist who specializes in childhood anxiety disorders, said that regardless of whether a child was diagnosed with anxiety or not, the way parents can help does not change. "We have seen many children referred for treatment in the last five years, and this seems to be increasing," the therapist told The Huffington Post UK. Parents can really do a lot at home to help a child who is suffering from anxiety.

If you notice that your child suffers from anxiety, you can be sure that you are not alone. Parents should only worry if they notice that their child's anxiety is having a significant effect on school or their relationships. Many children do not know what they feel when they are anxious, and this can be very scary and oppressive.

Identifying Signs of Anxiety in Your Child

I'll mention some examples where a mother connected the dots of some of the problems their child was suffering from, for example: bed-time problems, with the potential anxiety they might be suffering from through open, polite conversations and understanding.

"My son is almost 8 years old, and the first time I noticed his anxiety he was 4 1/2 years old," said Jordan Martin, 35, whose son is anxious before going to school. "I had to take him to school despite signs of anxiety, which were unusual [in his personality]: crying, shaking and holding his belly," said the mother. "I would drop him off at school and cry when I got home... It was very important to be consistent for him to go to school, but I felt terrible."

Martin cited as other signs of anxiety the child's fear of bed-time; he said that "bad things" could happen. "He cared about silly things like his school backpack not being at home, anything related to change," he added.

Salma Shah, whose 5-year-old daughter has anxious thoughts, often said that the behavior has been constant since she was a baby. "As a baby, I remember her turning her back on all the other babies and turning to me, distracting me by pointing at things," Shah explained.

"One of the main symptoms I noticed when she grew up was her attachment. If she had a 'playdate,' she would always be by my side and never spoke voluntarily to people, not even to family members with whom she had always had contact. "

Natasha Jones, 35, said the anxiety of Ella, her 7-year-old daughter, came when she was saddened to think about illness and death in the family. This was reinforced the first time she saw Harry Potter and Cinderella. The films sparked concern about death and the possibility of losing parents. "She was constantly worried if she was alone at home or with another family member," Jones explained. "The problem got worse if I was not at home. It affected her concentration on things like homework or playing, and she became very sensitive before bed, with frequent stomach pain. "

Now, how to help control a child's anxiety?

1. Divide Situations Into Small Portions

When a child is feeling anxious about a scenario, it is tempting to help her avoid it. But with that, he will never develop confidence. Instead, help them break up the situation they are having trouble with into small pieces and make lots of compliments with rewards as they tackle each 'piece' before moving to the next level.

For example, if a child is socially anxious, encourage him to attend small meetings and allow him to get used to it before attempting a slightly larger party.

2. Use Relaxation Techniques

Martin creates a "safe place" for the son, where he can feel protected and calm before going to bed. She talks to him using relaxation techniques, such as a soft tone and positive phrases.

The words parents can say during this relaxation should be the most appropriate for the child's needs. I use the first person, which works well, for example: 'Repeat in your mind:' I'm safe, I'm home wherever I am, it's okay.' A soft tone, with a light touch on the shoulder or chest, works well. And Martin is a great example of the same.

Be careful not to use negative words, so instead of saying, 'Do not be scared,' say something like: 'You're safe, all is calm, and all is well.'

3. Teach Breathing Techniques

Breathing, in general, helps anyone who is feeling anxious to draw attention to the action of breathing and not to the cause of worry. Controlling this can create a sense of calm and prevent future anxiety attacks. Martin said he uses these techniques to calm his son. "I use the technique of inhaling through the nose counting to four and then exhaling through the nose counting to four," he said.

The goal is for children to regain control over their emotions; so if they face a 'scary' or 'uncomfortable' situation, they can resort to safe and effective strategies, such as the powers of a superhero.

4. Stimulate A 'Happy Thought'

Martin says he tries to tell his son a statement positive every night before he goes to sleep and every morning before he goes to school - which is when he feels more anxious. "He now asks for this specifically," he said. "I think he feels safe and supported, knowing he can focus on this when he goes to sleep or on the way to school. My husband was the one who started with the 'happy thought.' My son asks, 'What is my happy thought?' ".

Encourage the children to choose their own happy memory because it is their mind, and only they can know what animates their spirit.

5. Prepare For Anxiety-Provoking Situations

"We have come to places or parties early, so my daughter has not to walk among a lot of people, "Shah said, explaining that the daughter feels anxious in social situations. She said that preparing for possible anxiety situations in advance allows the daughter to deal better with them. "She responds kindly to kindness," she added. "We also highly commend her when she actually attends a party or event to reinforce her achievement."

6. Over time, Expose Your Child to Different Circumstances

Shah said parents should never worry about the possible embarrassment of the child being "too attached." They should focus more on building trust in their children. Do not push them too hard. But kindly, over time, expose them to different circumstances that will get them out of their comfort zone.

7. Do Not Get Angry, Work As A Team

"We try to be understanding and recognize my daughter's problems," explained Jones. "We've done a lot of research to try out techniques that would suit Ella, and one of the best ways to reassure her is to talk to her. Telling her that she's not alone and that other children have the same fears, including me, is comforting. We work as a team, and she knows it will take time for her fear to go away".

8. Create A 'Book Of Worries'

To help children with long-term anxiety, you can create a" worries book," and through that, you can encourage them to see what things make them anxious - their triggers. Just in case they are old enough to do this, have them write their thoughts in a 'book of worries.' Jones said the daughter uses this technique, writing her thoughts into a "box of worries."

9. Talk To Other Parents

For parents who do not know how to help their children deal with anxiety or anxious thoughts, talking with other parents to know their techniques can give ideas. Sometimes the solution is closer than we think.

10. Seek Professional Help If Anxiety Persists

If anxiety does not improve over two or three months or is significantly affecting your child's ability to socialize or go to school, you must seek professional help. Therapists who specialize in children can be consulted privately or through their GP. For example, the British government recommends that children with social anxiety have 8-12 sessions of cognitive-behavioral therapy.

Children are anxious by nature. In the car, they ask every five minutes how much time is left to complete the trip. At school, they may experience belly pain on test days. At home, they hang around the kitchen until dinner is served. The willingness to anticipate situations and the excitement of what is to come is part of child development - but to a limit. When they start to generate suffering and get in the way of everyday life, it can be a sign of a bigger problem.

According to the American Association of Anxiety Disorders, between 9% and 15% of the population aged five to 16 suffers from the disorder, which is characterized by a set of physical reactions, psychological and behavioral that precede a real or imaginary situation.

Carolina Schneider Silva, a psychologist at the Santo Antônio Children's Hospital of Santa Casa de Misericórdia in Porto Alegre, explains that anxiety attacks are disproportionate reactions of children to the stimulus they receive, whatever they will be. In Julia's case, a single line served as a trigger.

Crises can be characterized by a sense of fear and apprehension, marked by a period of tension or discomfort in the face of some event considered dangerous, even if it does not offer real risk. When exaggerated, they may appear in the form of tachycardia, muscle tension, tremors, shortness of breath, fainting, and bowel problems.

Know the Signs, Treatments and Know What to Do

The symptoms of an anxiety disorder may arise suddenly or gradually. Possibly, so they go unnoticed by many parents.

External Stimuli

Childhood is a period of many changes, and the degree of anxiety goes through oscillations as the child grows. Whether at the beginning of the school year, in routine changes or changes in the family environment, external stimuli generate new sensations and emotions.

In this age group, there are two types of anxiety disorder most common: Generalized Anxiety Disorder (GAD) and Anxiety and Separation Disorder (ASD). Science cannot yet explain why some children develop the problem, but some factors seem fundamental:

- The development of anxiety disorders results from the interaction of multiple factors such as genetic inheritance, the temperament the psychiatrist Gustavo Teixeira, a member of the American Academy of Psychiatry for Childhood and Adolescence and author of books on the same subject.

Experts argue that the picture is also linked to the excess of stimuli that children currently receive. They are subjected to greater social and emotional pressure from both the family and the school, for example.

- It is necessary to know the children and to be alert to changes, be they physical or behavioral. The most common ways of expressing anxiety are through recurring concerns and difficult to control. Together, there may be restlessness, easy tiredness, difficulty concentrating, irritability, and trouble sleeping or staying asleep.

How To Deal With Behavior Disorder In School?

A school brings together students from completely different personalities. There are those quieter students, the more introspective, the communicators, and those who never obey the rules. In the latter case, delivering an activity in the classroom can be quite an exercise in patience. However, you need to be cautious with children because behavioral disorders are much more complex than a simple tantrum.

Early childhood education should be ready to welcome children in general, but it is true that the most questioning, for example, presents a challenge for the educator. When you are faced with a student who has such characteristics, the best way is to be able to deal with each particularity brought to the school environment.

What Are These Behaviors?

Conduct can be diverse and range from challenging questions to physical aggression in extreme cases. However, it is important to point out other behaviors that are related to the disorder referred to in this article: rule violation, disobedience in the classroom, bullying of the child to other colleagues and teachers; cries, impulsive actions, provocations, discussions, and school dropouts.

Preparation

No doubt, there are many parents and teachers who are not prepared to deal with such situations. However, warning children energetically is not a step to be taken, although many do. That's because the little ones can feel challenged and insist on the attitude that motivated the warning made.

How To Deal Then?

The common point of all ways of dealing with behavioral disorders is dialogue. It is important always to establish communication between the child and the adult. Ask the child, the reason for such disobedience and try to have the confidence of the little one. Of course, this is not so simple, but there are ways to reduce the causes of these behaviors:

- Family therapy: support groups that work to develop the relationship between parents and children are a great alternative. In this situation, experts advise parents to establish effective communication with the child and to show them the limits to be placed on the child's behavior.

- Psychological follow-up: the child who presents some behavioral disorder in school can also find ways to improve their relationship and interaction with the environments in which they are. Psychological counseling can mean a very good way for the little one, from the moment therapy can help you get along with everyone around you.

- Multidisciplinary team: nothing more indicated than to act together with a diversified team, that brings together therapists and school teachers in the search for the improvement of the child's behavior.

And The Parents?

Parents and guardians should establish a satisfactory communication with the pedagogical and therapeutic group in order to arrive at an adequate response to the disorder presented.

It is very important that everyone has patience with the child since the child must find trust and authority in adults. To act cautiously does not mean ceasing to impose limits. On the contrary, the limits are indispensable. Adequate follow-up and parental attention are important determinants of behavior disorder.

Chapter 19: How To Replace Punishment With Positive Parenting

A positive approach to parenthood implies an understanding of the child and of his or her behavior, paying attention to how the child feels. What does that mean practically? Seeing what is behind a child's behavior means seeing the real cause, understanding it, and offering the child an alternate solution to negative behavior.

Adults mostly only see the "final product" – the unwanted behavior that they want to correct, or a symptom of the real cause. If they want the child to learn something and that isn't working, it is up to adults to explain to the child the consequences of his negative behavior: natural consequences ("You are cold because you do not want to wear a sweater.") and logical consequences ("We are late for the birthday party because you wanted to play even though the clock was ringing and telling us it was time to go.").

Positive parenting requires a calm tone of voice with a previous agreement and an explanation of what is acceptable and what is not, as well as what will happen if the child does not adhere to the agreement. Positive parenting creates a space for learning without guilt, shame, and the fear of punishment.

Children learn by making a series of efforts and mistakes. The whole process of a child's upbringing and learning is a series of attempts and mistakes until they master some skills. The role of the parents in this process is to provide direction and leadership. You must be a teacher to your children first of all, but a patient one.

The part of the brain that is responsible for reason, logic, and the control of impulses is not fully developed until adolescence. "Immature" behavior is normal in "immature" human beings that have "immature" brains. This is a scientific fact and whatever you feel as a parent and however you behave in these situations, you will not change that.

Parenting is difficult and requires the patience to repeat the same thing hundreds of times. Being a child is also difficult because it requires strength and persistence to repeat the same thing hundreds of times until it is learned. This process cannot be accelerated, skipped, or eliminated. The only thing a parent can do is change their perspective and accept that some things are slow and annoying, and have to be repeated many times. Some parents have days when they feel discouraged because they have to repeat the same thing day after day. But that is also a great part of parenthood.

Children learn about the world from their parents, and learning isn't just about gathering information. One of the most important things in your child's process of learning is learning how to live in the society in which he or she is growing up and learning the rules to function in that society. Kids have to know when it is proper and better for them to limit their autonomy and self-expression and they have to know that they are able to do it. Then, they have to learn how to tolerate frustration and handle frustration, and to be consistent in spite of it.

Without the adequate limits in their environment, children feel agitated and unmanaged. Boundaries can be expressed as criticism and cause embarrassment or they can be uttered in a solid way - full of respect. Think about how you like to be spoken to and speak the same way to your child. Do you respond better to vigorous criticism or to respect, regard, and support? It's the same with your child.

If we allow them to, children will try to solve the problems they face in their development and upbringing. Parents often begin to scold or criticize the child, not expecting the child to attempt to solve the problem. If the parents were more patient, they would be surprised how much their children are actually capable of making conclusions and solving the problems they face.

Being heard is therapeutically powerful and allows us to think about things clearly and find a solution. The same goes for children. Sometimes it's enough just to listen to a child when they talk about the problems they are having because they often come up with solutions that resolve the problems.

Fear and control are effective in the short term, but a child can become either completely blocked in his development or can begin to provide resistance to parental pressure through defiance and rebellion. Depending on the type of interaction a child has with his or her parents, the child forms a picture of himself and a sense of self-reliance in his roles in life. A blocked, non-progressing child has a lesser perception of his value which can lead to isolation or to its opposite: aggressive and rebellious behavior.

Children should understand the importance of thoughts and emotions, not just behavior because it will enable them to function better in relationships with other people and to deal better with problems. That is why adequate control of their emotions is an important skill and one of the most important goals of parenting.

The words of parents and their assessments of a child are a mirror for that child. Children will see what their parents exhibit. That then becomes their picture of themselves and they live with that. That is why it is very important to be specific and accurate with criticism. Criticism should be expressed with body language which expresses regret rather than disapproval toward the child. A parental look full of condemnation and criticism will be internalized by the child, and we want to love and accept our children. This strong support for them will be the seed and the core of their happy life and success.

However, you shouldn't give your child unlimited freedom, you do need to discipline them, of course. But how? Disciplinary measures respond to the child and his abilities and support the child in developing self-discipline. Discipline aims to positively target children, recognizing individual values and building positive relationships. Positive discipline empowers children's faith in themselves and their ability to behave appropriately.

Discipline is training and orientation that helps children to develop limits, self-control, efficiency, self-sufficiency, and positive social behavior. Discipline is often misunderstood as punishment, especially by those who apply strict punishment in their endeavors to make changes to children's behavior. But discipline is not the same as punishment.

Instead of punishment, it is important for children to be provided with support in the development of self-discipline. Positive discipline shows adults as figures with authority that children give the opportunity to develop strategies to control their own behavior according to the age of the child. Parents should take e a positive approach to discipline, developing positive alternatives to punishment.

Education is based on establishing and building relationships with your child, and the basis of each relationship is acceptance, respect, and established boundaries. Setting the boundaries during your child's education is equally important as understanding, love, and support. In this way, children learn to be responsible for what is happening to them, they are helped to learn self-regulation of their feelings and behaviors, and they gain self-confidence, but also to feel the confidence and trust of their parents.

Children are not born with an awareness of what is good and what is not. This is knowledge that they adopt, and their parents are the ones who assist most in this. It's a tough job and children need the support of adults during this process. Parents just need to learn how to stay patient and calm and help their child to learn in the best way possible.

Tips and Solutions for Peaceful and Positive Parenting

Speak in a calm voice - Rather than shout, talk with your child. This will help you to understand how kids need to feel a bit more of your patience. The way you react always influences the way the child behaves. Use positive parenting because it is vital for a healthy relationship between you and your child.

Give yourself a break - Patience is time-consuming. Sometimes it's hard to understand why your child behaves in a certain way and what you can do to help them. Patience is difficult when you have no time and your child wants something from you. Patience is the power of understanding your child.

Try to understand your child - Understanding is the foundation of positive parenting and influences communication and respect. It is very easy to lose patience with a child you do not understand. Your toddler will always be a little nervous, tearful, angry, or just loud and not listening. However, you're a parent with unconditional love. If you always try to talk to your child from the basis of this unconditional love you will surely understand him better and become more patient.

Let your child be independent - If you really want to practice patience, put it to work in situations where you want your child to take on tasks for himself. Stop and allow the child to finish things. This is how the child will enjoy independence and you, at the same time, will learn to be more patient.

Find the fastest way to calm yourself down - This is one of the most important things to learn about patience. There are simple things you can do that can help you. For example, deep breathing. You can also count to 10, bake a cake, or something like that. You know what you can do to bring about quick relaxation.

Chapter 20: Building Resiliency

Deep Breathing Exercises

When we feel strong emotions of any kind, our breathing becomes heavy and erratic. But the opposite is also true. If our breathing is heavy and erratic, it's very difficult for us to relax. When you are doing any healing work with your Inner Child, it is important to be aware of breathing. Strong emotions can and will well up from within you. Childhood trauma is something that we bury for a reason. Breathing slowly, deeply, and mindfully brings our thoughts back to our breath, and therefore back to our body. Whenever we feel angry, sad, or frightened, returning you to your body will return you to the present moment. The danger is gone, but your feelings can be as intense as they were in the moment of crisis. Bringing yourself back to the body brings you back from the past moment of trauma to the present moment of peace and gives you the stability you need to transform from frightened child to comforting parent. Breathing mindfully keeps you in a tranquil physical space so that you can ask the Inner Child what is wrong, confront the wrongs you may have done as a child or an adult, and approach the conflicts you're having within yourself or out in the world with Love, Patience, and Forgiveness (Hanh, 2010).

Releasing Trapped Feelings

The feelings that most often accompany trauma and leave the biggest scars on the Inner Child are:

Anger

Guilt

Shame

Grief

Abandonment

Rejection

Neglect

Powerless

Hopeless

Trapped

Worthless

Burdened (Wallace, 2015).

In order to heal the Inner Child, these trapped feelings must be released. To do this, we must develop resiliency.

People who have experienced trauma respond in one of two ways: submit or rebound. When we submit to a traumatic experience, we essentially agree with the perpetrator. We believe that we, in some way, deserved what happened to us. As adults, this often presents as codependency. When your long-distance partner forgets to call you, you may feel angry, and then guilty for being angry. When your parents say something that humiliates or disrespects you, you hide your hurt and pretend to laugh it off. When we do this, we are not allowing ourselves to experience our feelings authentically. We are disconnected from the Inner Child. (O'Gorman and Oliver-Diaz, 2012).

When we rebound from trauma, on the other hand, we recognize that what happened to us is not about us, but about the perpetrator. Trauma is not, and never was, our responsibility. The only thing we own is how we respond when we are not loved, nurtured, or respected. Do you feel a deep sense of grief or abandonment when a partner files for divorce? Do you feel rejected or neglected when your child doesn't call to wish you a Merry Christmas? These feelings are absolutely warranted and appropriate. Overreactions are about **actions,** not feelings. When you feel neglected, do you choose to write a nasty Facebook post about how the next generation is irresponsible and disconnected? What if, instead, you sent your child a text message: "Hey, Merry Christmas kiddo! I didn't hear from you yesterday – I hope everything's ok." The first response is, dare I say, childish? The first reaction is a spontaneous age regression, your Inner Child throwing up its defenses so that it doesn't have to feel the pain of rejection.

Resiliency is the ability to grow out of difficult or trying situations. It's not about being stoic or invincible. It's not about not feeling negative feelings. It's about choosing to acknowledge negative feelings without judgement and release them in authentic, harmonious ways. Resiliency is the inevitable result of a happy, whole Inner Child. When we have successfully healed the traumatic wounds of the past, we are better able to face future problems with strength, courage, and compassion.

Chapter 21: Making Your Child Feel Safe And Secured

It is quite imperative for a child's healthy development to feel important and secured. Healthy self-esteem is a child's armor against the challenges of the world. Certainly, children who feel good and safe about themselves seem to have an easier time handling conflicts and resisting negative influences.

They tend to smile more readily and enjoy life. These kids seem to be more realistic and generally optimistic.

It has also been shown that children who feel important are well-rounded, respectful, honored and integrity. They excel in academics, extracurricular activities and hobbies and develop healthy relationships with other kids.

In fact, children who do not feel important or cherished have low self-esteem, and challenges can become sources of major anxiety and frustration. Furthermore, children who think poorly of themselves have a hard time finding a way of solving problems, and may become passive, withdrawn, or even depressed.

Parents are the biggest influence in their child feeling important, valued, worthy and safe. Always remember that wherever you may be, you should commend your child for a job well done, and also for putting in a valiant effort. Praise the good traits they naturally possess, and help them find ways to learn from their mistakes and failures.

Distance Parenting could be very taunting. Be honest and sincere in your praising your children. Help them realize that you also suffer from self doubt and occasionally can make mistakes, but that you know that you are important, valued and loved by them.

However, when you nurture your own self-esteem and importance, your child or children will learn to do the same. So parents, be sure to lead by example and steer clear of demeaning yourselves or engaging in activities that lower self-worth or significance. Your child may have inaccurate or irrational beliefs about themselves, their abilities or their traits might vary. As parents, accentuating the positive things about your child, and encouraging the child to set realistic expectations and standards will be a soothing cushion.

Help them identify traits or skills they'd like to improve and help them come up with a game plan for accomplishing that goal. Parents should encourage their children to become involved in cooperative activities that foster a sense of teamwork and accomplishment.

Through these and other positive, affirming activities, the children will surely develop strong sense of self importance, value and worthy which will carry them into their adult years.

Most of us recognize the continuing escalation of violence around us, due to intolerance, and many of us blame it on somebody else. Parents teach their children, all the time, and when one of us displays "road rage," while our child is in the car, we teach a brand new skill set. Although, road rage is inappropriate behavior at any time, and can get you killed, most children who are exposed to it will duplicate the actions of their parents, when they are old enough to drive.

So, the first step to take is to set an example for your kid to follow and possibly, use some of the ideas here for yourself improvement. Studies show that anger causes atherosclerosis which is the build-up of plaques in the arteries. It is a major factor in developing high blood pressure, heart disease, heart attack, and eventually, premature death. Also, during a "temper tantrum," adrenaline and blood pressure levels rise beyond normal. This behavior is more dangerous to parent's bodies due to the normal catabolism already existing in the body.

Now, you may be convinced that anger can kill you, but let's look at one more factor. You could hurt someone else, find yourself in prison, or get yourself killed due to inciting violence against others. There are other people, who are having difficulty dealing with anger management too. So, "two wrongs can never be right they say."

Going back to the children, children need some time to exercise their bodied because they are naturally full of energy. If you look at all other species, you will see the same behavioral pertain. We cannot drug our pets when they display youthful exuberance.

Parents must always remember that children have to run, jump, and shout. So let them play in the back yard, in a park, and get them involved in sports, Yoga, dance, or martial arts. You will never regret letting your child enjoy life and constructively learn in the process, by just trying to be a kid.

For all of us, there is a time to be quiet and a time to shout. Children need years to learn this, so let's keep them active in the process. Keep them away from the television as much as possible, Internet, and video games, except for "rainy days" or school research work. Coloring books, board games, and reading are also good activities for rainy days.

If you have the space and environment, a heavy bag is a great tool for letting anger out. You and your child can use it together. You can learn to punch and kick it, for the aerobic benefits, as well.

In fact, if you have a friend who is a boxer or martial artist, you could get some pointers from him /her. After just a 20-minute session, I guarantee you and your child will have dealt with the anger with little or none left.

Teach your child forgiveness by your own example. I am not asking you to let people "walk all over you." However, let grudges go; life is really too short to keep a feud running in your vein for a long time.

You can also control your child's "circle of friends," just by getting him or her involved in, group activities such as: League sports, dance, yoga, or martial arts. The parents who have their children in these activities want the best for them and are willing to sacrifice their time, or money, to get it going. This will keep your child busy, happy, and active, with a pre-selected crowd of friends, who have parents that care. This is a "win – win" situation and well worth the investment.

This is not to say that every child you run into, at these functions, will be perfect, but most of the kids must have come from well-structured families. In the above mentioned activities, all of them are disciplined and structured, adult-supervised back home and rules for behavior are in place. This form of organization becomes a habit and your child will follow these guidelines, and bring them to your home.

In addition, you should have your child take care of a pet or a plant, every day. Children love to care for animals or plants, but they still need supervision. The result of this will be that your child learns compassion towards others.

Chapter 22: Single Mom With Toddler - Cutting Toxic Tv Time

Like most American parents, a single mom home alone with a toddler will probably seat his toddler comfortably on a baby chair and turn on the TV so the kid can watch his favorite cartoon channel while he does his house chores or attend to some personal calling. It is a fact that parents make use of the television to baby sit for them or use it as a pacifier.

What these parents don't know (or refuse to know) is that TV is toxic to infants and toddlers 2 years old and below. TV viewing for infants and toddlers robs them the chance to develop their own creative minds. It makes the kids too dependent on the boob tube for entertainment and prevents them from engaging in creative plays.

According to an advisory issued by the American Academy of Pediatrics, infants and toddlers watching too much TV negatively impacts their cognitive and language development and disturbs their regular sleeping patterns. Their study has also linked too much TV exposure during the first two years of the baby's life to greater health risks such as obesity, aggressive behavior, and ADHD.

ADHD, or Attention Deficit Hyperactivity Disorder, is a common psychiatric disorder affecting children. 9% of American children and 4.1% of American adults have been diagnosed with ADHD the symptoms of which include lack of focus, difficulty in paying attention, hyper activity, and difficulty in controlling behavior.

On the average, American children aged 1 to3 years old watch television 2 to 3 hours a day which by AAP standards is already child toxic and more than enough to put the child at risk of having the symptoms mentioned earlier. Unfortunately, the AAP stopped short at giving parents a warning and has not offered viable alternatives TV for entertaining or babysitting toddlers while their parents are busy with their chores.

This should not dampen your interest because there are really a lot of alternatives besides TV that can keep babies and toddlers entertained why you are busy doing something else. Do not forget that babies and toddlers are self-learners and they learn fast. They have the ability to create and engage in inner-directed plays - which in effect serves as the foundation of their learning.

We mistakenly think that there is always that need to stimulate a child or keep him entertained and so we do what we always do – put him in front of a TV – because that's what an adult will do to entertain themselves. The fact is we are unnecessarily occupying the baby's time and inhibit his natural urge to engage in his own activities and discover the world in his own terms.

The baby has the capacity to create and engage in his own independent play to entertain himself. Screen time prevents him from doing this. And worst, with screen time, we are not only branding his brains but we are also enslaving him to the boob tube while impairing his creative development.

Because infants can naturally initiate their own thoughts and activities, all we need to do is support and encourage them to cultivate these abilities- not with screen time, for God's sake – but by just letting him be. Simply give him play space and routinely leave him there – watching on the side of course. Babies learn best if we leave them to do their own thing. And as they grow older, all we need to do is to merely supply them with things they can use to self create their own independent plays. When they start to get bored with their own plays that would be the time to suggest what they can do.

Do not forget that not so long ago (before TV was invented) parents were able to keep their kids busy while they wash the dishes, clean the house, and attend to a hundred other household chores. It wasn't difficult then. It shouldn't be difficult now. Unless you want your kid to have branded brains, then it is best to heed the warnings of the child experts and keep them away from television — at least, during the first two years of their lives.

If you want some TV-free ideas on how to keep your toddlers pre-occupied and entertained as you go about your chores here they are:

Finger "Painting" (From Love Some)

This activity is perfect for 1 year old toddlers and up. The idea of finger painting may scare the wits out of you but this finger painting activity is mess-free and you won't need to keep a roll of paper towels ready. Get a zip lock bag and put several blobs of washable finger paint in it. Force the air out, lock, and seal with tape. Your toddler will enjoy pressing the blobs of paint and create different shapes for hours.

One Boy Band

This activity is good for 3 to 6 year old toddlers. Get your kid to bring out all his toy instruments. Line them up in a row and challenge your kid to create different compositions while going up and down the line of instruments and playing them. You can also challenge him to try and play two instruments simultaneously.

Make a Ball Maze (from A Happy Wanderer)

This activity is good for 2 year old and up toddlers. Make a maze using a large cardboard box and a lot of paper towel rolls. Cut the paper towel rolls in two and glue them (cascading down) the sides of the cardboard box. Let it dry and prop it up with a chair or anything to keep it tilted and in place. Give your kid some balls, or toy cars, or anything that rolls and let him drop them one at a time down the maze. This will keep him pre-occupied for hours.

If you are resourceful enough, you can find tons of these TV-free ideas on how to keep your toddlers entertained. Just keep on searching the net and select the ideas that are suitable to you and your child.

If you can't find the time to do this, then take out your iPhone and start downloading kid stuff applications like 'Wheels on the Bus', 'Smack Talk, and 'Scribble Lite' from the iPhone store. You will also find a lot of learn-to-read applications there. Teach your toddler how to play these games and it will keep him busy for hours. The only problem is you may not be able to get back your iPhone from him.

Conclusion

Parents need to set high standards with clear consequences when raising teenagers. These standards need to be well understood by the targeted teens who are also involved in the negotiation. However, it is not just about high standards; they wrap their approach with love, warmth, and the involvement to steer their teens to the right direction.

As opposed to popular belief, teens want to spend more time with their parents, a fact that has been made clear in this ebook. Good parenting practices require that you schedule adequate time with your teen and get fully engaged with him or her during this time.

It is also clear from this ebook that at teenage, the kids are developing their unique personalities and are likely to experiment and seek approvals from people close to them. They need a lot of guidance, and this is best done by establishing standards and expectations.

The teenagers need to be who they are, but you must guide ever one of their steps as they define their identities. As the parent, your role is not to model them to who you want them to be, but rather guide them to successfully become what they want to be.

It is clear that the most critical dangers a young boy or girl is likely to face as they try to find their identity are premature sex that results in unwanted pregnancies and sexually transmitted diseases and alcohol and substance abuse.

However, all these can be avoided with proper guidance. The book is dedicated to equipping parents with the skills they need to parent the teenagers. In this Ebook, you have been taken through the threats teenagers face, how to talk to teenagers and offer guidance, how to detect signs of abuse, neglect and how to deal with the challenges the teenagers face every day.

If you know of anyone else who may benefit from the informative tips presented in this book, please help me inform them of this book. I would greatly appreciate it.

Thanks again for your support and good luck!

www.ingramcontent.com/pod-product-compliance
Lightning Source LLC
Chambersburg PA
CBHW072004070526
44583CB00015B/1325